The People's Palace

The People's Palace

Parliament in Modern Australia

DAVID SOLOMON

MELBOURNE UNIVERSITY PRESS
1986

First published 1986
Typeset by Abb-typesetting Pty Ltd, Collingwood, Victoria
Printed in Australia by
The Dominion Press–Hedges & Bell, Victoria, for
Melbourne University Press, Carlton, Victoria 3053
U.S.A. and Canada: International Specialized Book Services
P.O. Box 1632, Beaverton OR 97075
United Kingdom, Europe, Middle East, Africa:
HB Sales
Enterprise House, Ashford Road, Ashford, Middlesex
England TW15 1XB

This book is copyright. Apart from any fair dealing for the purposes of private study, research, criticism or review, as permitted under the Copyright Act, no part may be reproduced by any process without written permission. Enquiries should be made to the publisher.

© David Solomon 1986

National Library of Australia Cataloguing-in-Publication entry

Solomon, David.
  The people's palace.
  Includes index.
  ISBN 0 522 84318 2.
  1. Australia. Parliament. I. Title.
328.94

For Jocelyn

Contents

Illustrations

Acknowledgements

I would like to express my thanks to the many people who helped produce the book. First, the Publications Subcommittee of the Commonwealth Parliament's Library Committee, which commissioned me to write it as one of the three major works in the Parliament's bicentennial publications project. Second, the Parliamentary Librarian, Hillas MacLean, who helped to make publication about as easy as could be. Third, the many Ministers and Opposition frontbenchers, and backbenchers on both sides of both Houses, and Senators in the smaller parties, who provided me with essential information and guidance. And fourth, the many public servants, parliamentary servants, journalists and others associated with the Parliament who contributed information, advice and assistance. The photograph of Parliament House on the cover was provided by the Australian Tourist Commission. Some illustrative material was previously printed in *House of Representatives Practice*, and I am grateful for permission to use this. Geoff Pryor responded enthusiastically to a last-minute request to provide cartoons and drawings which would help put everything in perspective.

CHAPTER 1

Introduction

Parliament is both the symbol of Australian democracy and the central and pivotal institution of that democracy. It is parliament which makes the laws under which the country is governed. It is from parliament that the nation's political leaders are chosen. It is Parliament that provides the stage for the testing of political parties and their policies. Parliament occupies a unique place in the political system. It stands between the Australian people and their Government. But as a link and a bridge—not as an impenetrable and impersonal barrier. It is through the election of Members of Parliament that governments are selected by the people—the prize going to the party or parties which wins a majority of seats in the House of Representatives. But parliament does not go into limbo once a Prime Minister and his Ministers take over. The Parliament has many tasks to perform between elections, including questioning and checking the government, keeping it aware of public concerns and attitudes, and providing the government with the financial and legal means of running the nation. Most importantly it provides a two-way channel for contact between 'us' and 'them'—between the people and their government. And ultimately the Parliament and its members have the power to decide whether a particular Government or Prime Minister continue as the Government or Prime Minister. A Prime Minister can be dismissed by the members of his parliamentary political party. A Government can be overturned if it cannot hold together its majority in the House of Representatives in the Parliament.

The Parliament also has great symbolic importance. Its members were extremely conscious of this when, over a period of about a decade, they decided on the siting and building of a new Parliament House to replace the building first opened in Canberra in

1927. The new Parliament House was scheduled to be finished and opened in 1988, as the major event celebrating 200 years of European settlement of Australia. The symbolic place of the Parliament was much debated for the many years it took to decide where the new building would be. The choices were on Capital Hill, at the apex of the parliamentary triangle in Walter Burley Griffin's prize-winning town-plan of Canberra; by the lake-side, on the line between Capital Hill and the War Memorial; or on Camp Hill, a small area immediately behind the first Parliament House. Those who thought it should be by the lake argued that it should be down by the people, and that the Capital Hill site would be undemocratic, in that people should not have to crawl up a hill to see politicians. The Camp Hill argument was based around the economic desirability (and therefore the political popularity in saving money) of retaining some use of the present building for parliamentary purposes, but Camp Hill was thought to be too low and too small for a substantial building. The Capital Hill's supporters sometimes argued that people ought to be able to look up to their national parliament (in a physical sense as well as metaphorically). As it turned out, the design chosen for the Capital Hill site will allow people both to look up to the new Parliament, and particularly to the giant flag which will dominate it, as well as being able to walk over the top of the building, while their political representatives work away beneath them.

The notion of parliamentary government has a long history and has gone through many changes. The first British Parliaments consisted of the King and his Lords. Then, gradually, the more wealthy landowners were able to take their place as the 'Commons' though in Britain the common working-man and woman were not able to vote for the Parliament until comparatively recently. In Australia, the colonies were first run by Governors appointed by the British Government. Pressures from the free settlers forced the Governors to appoint Councils to assist them in determining policies, and self-government was won by the larger colonies in the 1850s. They rapidly introduced voting for all adult men, though until the turn of the century the people who owned property generally had more than one vote. Women won the vote at about the turn of the century—twenty-five years ahead of their sisters in Britain.

The Commonwealth of Australia was created in 1901 at the very time that the last of the modern range of democratic processes were being introduced in the Australian colonies, and well before similar developments in most other countries. As a result, the

Commonwealth Parliament has always been a fully democratic body which has had to be sensitive to the demands of the whole of the public—and not simply a powerful sector of it. Because everyone has a vote, politicians need to pay attention to everyone in their electorates.

The Australian Parliament has many unique features. Australian parliamentarians, concerned about their popularity, and what might happen at the next election (and elections are held very frequently), have allowed the Commonwealth Parliament to develop in ways which are not always the same as overseas parliaments. They have adopted procedures which allow them to remain in as close touch as possible with their voters, despite the problems of distance and Canberra's remoteness. They were very quick, for example, to agree to the broadcasting of parliamentary proceedings, forcing the government-funded Australian Broadcasting Commission (later known as the Australian Broadcasting Corporation) to devote one of its two city networks to broadcasting the proceedings of one of the Houses whenever the Parliament was sitting.

Australian parliamentary elections serve two main purposes. They directly allow voters to choose someone to represent them in Parliament; and indirectly they allow voters to select the government which is to run the country for the next three years. Parliament then becomes an intermediary between the voters and the government. This is quite unlike the presidential system in the United States, for example, where people vote directly for the President, and separately for the Congress—that is, the American people vote separately for their government (the President) and their equivalent of Parliament (the Congress).

The Australian system involves an election in which there is a contest for government between the Labor Party on one side, and the Liberal and National parties on the other (these have been the major party groupings for most of this century, though there have been some changes of name and composition on the non-Labor side). The Liberal and Labor parties both go into the election with a leader who is seeking to be Prime Minister. The people do not have the chance to choose directly between those leaders, however. Instead they have to vote for a member of the Labor Party, the Liberal Party or the National Party (to vote for a candidate who is a member of a smaller party or an independent is to opt out of a direct vote in the contest between the parties seeking to govern the country—but the voting system provides for every voter to express a preference between the major parties somewhere on the ballot paper—see Chapter 13). The major parties contest almost every electorate for the House of Representatives, and the winner—the party which becomes the Government and whose leader becomes Prime Minister—is the party which gets enough of its candidates elected to have a majority of votes in the House of Representatives. The other members of the Government—the Ministers—are elected by the party members in the Parliament (in the case of the Labor Party) or chosen by the Prime Minister (in the case of the Liberal–National party coalition). But all of them—Prime Minister and Ministers—continue to serve as Members of Parliament as well as performing their functions as Ministers in the Government. What the Government does and what the Parliament does are two quite separate things. Parliament makes the laws; the Government carries them out and is responsible for maintaining law and order, relations with other countries and with the states, and for managing the economy, the public service and the defence forces. But Parliament does not just wash its hands of its responsibilities in relation to the Government. The House of Representatives has the power to change the Government if it is not satisfied with its performance, and to do so without forcing an election. The last time this happened in Australia was in 1941 when the Fadden–Menzies Government was defeated in the House of Representatives to be replaced by a Labor Government. An election was not held until two years later: it confirmed the Labor Party in power, and virtually destroyed Menzies' party.

The role of Parliament

It is not always easy for the casual visitor to Parliament to be sure what the MPs[1] and Senators are doing and what they are trying to achieve. Often what is really happening in the Parliament is disguised by methods of saying and doing things which seem to make very little sense. (They are largely copied from procedures used by the British Parliament hundreds of years ago.) There is a special parliamentary language (for example, MPs are 'Honourable Members' and are referred to by the electorates they represent, not by their own names). There are special ways of behaving and counting votes and a complex set of rules (slightly different in each House) controlling the way the Parliament goes

---

[1] MP is a common abbreviation for any Member of any Parliament, but in this book it is used in its strictest (Australian) sense to mean a Member of the House of Representatives.

about its business. (These are discussed in more detail in Chapter 6 and Chapter 10.)

Behind all the pomp and often confusing behaviour, the Parliament is performing a series of functions which are crucial to the democratic process.

1. *Legislating*

The main function of the Parliament is to consider and pass laws. This has to be done through the agreement of both the Houses of Parliament and because the Government these days does not often control the Senate, the process can involve real disagreements and the need for compromises. All but a few laws which are passed by the Parliament are drawn up by the Government and the public service, to bring government policies into effect. But the Parliament does not have to 'rubber stamp' them. It can change them and it can even reject them altogether. (The law-making process is discussed in detail in Chapter 10.)

2. *Scrutinising the Government*

This activity might be summarised as 'keeping the Government honest', a function which in one way or another is carried out by all MPs and Senators, from all parties. The Parliament is able to question the members of the Government about all their actions and their policies, and about the effects and results of those policies when they are implemented. There are a series of devices available to the members of the Parliament to perform this scrutiny of government. The most apparent is Question Time, when any Opposition or backbench MP or Senator can question any Minister about the activities of the Minister, or of his department, or of any other branch of the Government for which he is responsible. Ministers and their senior departmental officials also have to answer in person to any parliamentary committee which might affect their administration. Such investigations are carried on twice a year by Senate committees which inquire into the estimates of departmental expenditures which are listed in the Budget. In addition, the Public Accounts Committee carries out an investigation whenever it is told by the Auditor-General of faulty financial administration, and the Public Works Committee investigates any major expenditures proposed on new buildings. These activities provide a means by which the Parliament is able to exercise a very real measure of supervision over the spending processes of the Government. A third way in which Ministers may have to answer to the Parliament is when individual MPs raise complaints in debates in the Parliament—and there are many opportunities for MPs and Senators to raise such issues. The questioning of Ministers by parliamentarians takes place in a less formal way outside the parliamentary chambers—in Ministers' offices, in the Government party room, and even less formally in the corridor or the library or the refreshment rooms. Ministers cannot ignore such questioning because they know that they can always be subjected to public criticism at a later time in the Parliament if they do nothing to correct a particular mistake or answer a special grievance.

3. *Providing a political stage*

Parliament often seems like theatre. Its principal actors read their lines and act their parts with varying degrees of skill and dash. There is drama, humour, pathos. There is a colourful backdrop and some ancient costumes. Occasionally there is even movement. Of course it is not always exciting, even to the political devotee. And for a great deal of the time, when it seems that the stage has been taken over by the bit players, or members of the chorus, or even by the understudies, no one really seems very interested in the performance at all. But for the highlights, the critics are ever present, writing their reviews for evening television, for radio, and for the morning papers. And the performers, like all actors, avidly read their notices to see how their performances have been rated.

Some of what happens in Parliament really is meant to provide something like a staged confrontation. There genuinely is meant to be a display of the wares of the Government and the Opposition and the individual virtues of various politicians. That takes place in a variety of ways. Perhaps the most significant is Question Time, which tends to be concerned more with the display of political attitudes (and the attempted destruction of one's political opponents) than with information seeking. An even more formal debating confrontation occurs when the Opposition moves a censure or motion of no confidence. This is rarely done in the expectation that a vote will favour the Opposition's point of view, but to win space in the media for the criticisms which the Opposition is directing at a particular Minister or government action or policy. This attention-seeking is also one of the reasons for rowdiness and what appears to be misbehaviour. Yelling across the Chamber, using so-called unparliamentary language, confronting the Speaker—all these are ways in which MPs and Oppositions can draw attention to particular complaints or particular issues.

4. Determining the Government

The state of the parties in the House of Representatives deter-mines which party forms the Government, and to a very large extent whether that party retains Government. A party with a clear majority in its own right, needs only to remain internally cohesive (that is, to avoid splitting, or losing any individual party members) to retain control of the House of Representatives and of the Government. In the first years of the Commonwealth Parliament, when there were three major parties vying for office, the party which became the Government was the one which was able to persuade one of its opponents that in return for its support, it would push certain programs which they both approved of. Failure to deliver meant withdrawal of support, and the defeat of that Government in the House. The same applies to a far lesser extent to Governments formed by the coalition of the Liberal and National parties. They have a coalition agreement, which spells out how they will deal with such things as the allocation of ministerial portfolios and the extent to which either party can veto joint decisions. Any breakdown of such agreements could again lead to defeat in the House. More rarely, a Government may depend on the support of independents to retain its majority in the House. That was the situation in 1941 when a change in the attitude of independents resulted in a change in Government.

The Senate has no part to play in the formation of governments, but in 1975 it in effect asserted a right to control the continued existence of a Government, when it refused to pass the Govern-ment's budget. The intervention of the Governor-General in the crisis resulted in an election being held. There is still division among the various political parties about the desirability of the Senate exercising any such life or death powers over a government which owes its creation to its control of the House of Representatives. The Senate has on several occasions voted no confidence in Ministers who were Senators. The Ministers have not felt obliged to resign their offices, nor has the Senate attempted to force them to do so. It appears that the Senate retains its ultimate power over Governments to control the fate of the whole Government, but not individual members of it.

5. Keeping the public in touch with Parliament

Much of what the Parliament does is an effort to publicise the current political debate—or so much of it as actually occurs in the Parliament itself. The grand political theatre, mentioned above, needs an audience, if it is to achieve anything. The confrontations of Question Time, no-confidence motions, and ministerial pronouncements, are all intended to communicate views and ideas to the public generally. Much of the work of committees is also concerned with spreading knowledge to the public of particular problem areas—a committee dealing with environmental problems is intended to make the public aware of the nature of particular environmental problems as much as it is with coming up with answers to those problems. The Parliament relies on the fact that it is being broadcast to get some of its message across. It relies even more on the newspaper, television and radio journalists who inhabit the parliamentary Press Gallery to publicise what the Parliament is doing and what its members are saying.

6. *Keeping Parliament in touch with the public*

The Parliament has a series of devices which are specifically designed to keep open channels of communication between the public and the Parliament itself (and through the Parliament, the Government). Some of these are ancient, like the right to petition the Parliament. Each year, tens of thousands of people sign petitions which are received by the Parliament, and sent on to appropriate Ministers. The Parliament also provides time for its backbench and opposition members to raise problems or grievances which are felt by individual members of the public. Parliamentary Committees positively seek out (through public advertisements) complaints or submissions from members of the public and from pressure groups or others who might be interested in particular problems being investigated. The Parliament has also established an ombudsman, to whom people can complain about their treatment by public authorities—complaints which whether successfully dealt with or not, are passed on to the Parliament for information by the ombudsman. And most members of Parliament are very much alive to the general political complaints of their constituents—the reaction of members of their parties and of the public generally to whatever the Government is doing or not doing and whatever the party happens to be proposing or opposing.

The Government in Parliament

An unusual feature of the Australian political system is the close contact between members of the Government, and the other Members of the Parliament. This is enhanced by the physical location of Ministers' offices in the Parliament building, and the requirement for Ministers to be ready to attend Parliament at any time when it is sitting. This is not the usual pattern in Britain, for example, where the Prime Minister lives and works at Number 10 Downing Street (and the Chancellor of the Exchequer at Number 11), and visits to the Parliament are comparatively rare—in Britain the Prime Minister attends two short sessions of Question Time each week, whereas in Australia the Prime Minister is expected to be present and answer questions throughout Question Time every day of the week when the Parliament is sitting. In the United States, the President only attends the Congress to make an occasional address to it, and the members of his Cabinet attend it essentially for the purpose of trying to persuade Congressional committees to adopt their proposals. In the United States the only member of the Cabinet who may be a member of the Congress is the Vice President, who presides over the Senate.

In Canberra, Ministers spend more time in Parliament House than do any other members of the Parliament. The Ministers use their Parliament House offices even when the Parliament is not sitting. The Cabinet room is located immediately next to the Chamber of the House of Representatives. The Prime Minister works in a suite of offices next to the Cabinet room, not from his official residence which does not contain any real office facilities. When Parliament is sitting Ministers have to attend every Question Time and be ready to leave their offices and go into the Chamber at a minute's notice to vote or help make up a quorum. Their presence in Parliament House makes them available to every member of the Parliament, Government or Opposition. Although Ministers tend to have a busy timetable of meetings which keeps up throughout the Parliamentary day, they can always be approached by Members anxious to raise a problem or argue a case. This can be seen to happen even in the Parliamentary chambers, while votes are being counted.

Federalism and Responsible Government

Those who wrote the Australian Constitution were 19th century colonial politicians, who had been brought up in the traditions of the British political system as it then existed and as it had been adapted by the various Australian colonies as they achieved self-government from the mid-1850s onwards. While they wanted to create a united Australian nation which reflected British political values and institutions, most of them also wanted to preserve what they then had—the governments of the colonies which they had helped to build. They were not radical or revolutionary men (there were no women at all). When they met in a series of conventions from 1891 to 1897 to draft and adopt a constitution for a nation which would cover the whole continent, they accepted that the old colonial boundaries would remain and that the parliaments in Sydney, Melbourne, Brisbane, Adelaide, Hobart and Perth would continue to function and control most of the activities of the peoples in their respective territories.

They had several examples on which they could base their new political system. The Unites States and Canada had both been created by the process called federation, which preserved the separate identities of the States which were to be combined to form the new nation. The Canadians showed that the new federal system could operate with a system of government based on the British parliamentary system (the Westminster system) where the Government was chosen from among elected Members of Parliament. The United States example showed the means by which the smaller States could preserve their integrity despite being caught up in a new nation alongside States very much larger than themselves. This was done through providing that they should have equal representation in the new upper House of the Parliament, the Senate, which would have very strong powers so that it could prevent the 'popular' or 'people's' house (the House of Representatives) from ignoring States' needs and rights, particularly the needs of the smaller States. They fixed the size of the House of Representatives at about twice the size of the Senate. This meant that for the first Parliament, New South Wales, the largest, and Western Australia and Tasmania, the smallest States, would each have six Senators, but because the size of state representation in the House of Representatives went according to population, New South Wales would have 26 members in the House but Western Australia and Tasmania five (the permanent minimum representation for a State in the House).

There was never any doubt in the minds of all but a few of the politicians who created the Commonwealth that Australia would remain part of the British Empire under the Queen. The Queen was to be represented in Australia by a Governor-General, just as in the colonies she was represented by a Governor. The system of government which already existed in the colonies (or States, as they were to be called when the Commonwealth of Australia came into being) was not going to change under the new Federal Constitution. The States would retain their previous colonial constitutions, and parliaments and governments. All that would happen would be that some of their powers would be taken over by the new national Parliament and Government. Their main concern was that the national Government would look after defence, international trade and tariffs, and the postal and telegraph system. The general expectation seemed to be that the States would be more important than the new Commonwealth, and exercise more power—though most of the leading politicians who helped create the new nation moved from colonial to national politics very quickly, and set about enhancing the powers of the national Government.

Under the new system, the Commonwealth was headed by the Governor-General, representing the Queen, and there was a Parliament consisting of the Senate and the House of Representatives. The Government (headed by a Prime Minister) would be formed from the party or parties controlling a majority of votes in the House. At the State level, the formal head of Government remained the Governor, representing the Queen, and again there were two Houses of Parliament (though the State Parliaments had the ability to change their own constitutions and Queensland later abolished its upper House). Again, Governments (headed by a Premier) were to be formed by the party or parties able to control the lower or more popular House of Parliament.

The new Federal Constitution was deliberately made difficult for future generations to change, again because of fears that the smaller States might be swamped by the pressures of the larger States, and because it had taken so much effort to work out the compromises between different interest groups and different political viewpoints which were enshrined in the Constitution.

Although the general structures of the Australian, Canadian and United States federations are similar, although the party systems in Australia, Canada and Britain are similar, and although Commonwealth and State political systems are almost identical, there are in fact very great differences between the way Parliaments and Governments operate in those different countries and even within Australia. The relationships between Parliament and Government, and between Parliament and people, are decided less by the grand design of a political system than by minor variations, by quirks of history, by the contributions of individuals and by accident. Small changes in the rules often result in substantial changes in the way a system works (as any football or cricket fan would appreciate). And the system is continually changing.

In Canberra, developments since the beginning of the 1970s

have resulted in a Parliament which has become increasingly responsive to the people who elect it, and Governments which have become extremely responsive to the demands of the individual Members of the Parliament. In that sense, both Government and Parliament have become increasingly democratic.

CHAPTER 2

The Two Houses of the Parliament

The Constitution makes the two Houses of the Australian Parliament very different institutions, and over time they have come to have quite distinct functions. The House of Representatives has approximately twice the number of Members as does the Senate—148 in the House, and 76 in the Senate. Members of the House represent areas which are determined according to the number of voters, whereas Senators are elected to represent the whole of a State or Territory. Elections for the House of Representatives are held at least once every three years. Senators are elected for six-year periods, though their terms are staggered so that half the Senate has to face an election every three years. Members of the House of Representatives are elected under a preferential voting system. Senators are elected through a proportional representation system.

The House of Representatives

The House of Representatives is sometimes referred to as the 'lower' House, or the 'popular' House of the Parliament. It is the equivalent to the House of Commons in England, which was called the lower House by contrast to the House of Lords, which consisted of the upper classes of society. It is called the 'popular' House because it most directly represents the people of Australia. The voting system is such that it is as close as possible to the ideal democratic notion of 'one man-one vote' and 'one vote-one value'. Each Member of the House of Representatives represents approximately the same number of voters (about 65 000 in 1985). It is because the members of the House perform this function of giving equal representation to the people of Australia that it has the function of providing the Government.

Because of the comparative fairness of the electoral system used for the House of Representatives, the split between the major parties in the House very closely represents the national political feeling at the time of the election, though the system does tend to exaggerate any disparity between the main parties, and almost eliminate the possibility of parties which have only small but widespread support from gaining representation in the House of Representatives. The party or parties which control a majority of the votes in the House of Representatives—that is, those which won a majority of the electorates—will normally have won slightly more than a majority of votes throughout Australia. In the past there have been several occasions when a party or parties has won Government without winning as many votes as its opponents; this would be most unlikely to happen under the latest electoral laws (see Chapter 13 for a more detailed account of the electoral system).

Parliament does not govern the country and is not supposed to. The business of government is in effect delegated to a committee which consists of the leaders of the party or parties which controls the majority of votes in the House of Representatives (that is, the Cabinet and the Ministry). The Constitution requires that the Ministers who form any Government have to be Members of either the House of Representatives or the Senate—or to become Members within three months. That partial exemption was included in the Constitution to allow the first Government of the Commonwealth, in 1901, to hold office until the election was held—the new Government then being formed from the successful party at that election. However, the 'three months' provision also proved useful in 1968 after the death of the then Prime Minister, Harold Holt. The Liberal Party selected John Gorton to be its leader and to become Prime Minister. But Gorton was a Senator, and everyone accepted that he had to become a member of the House of Representatives if he was to be Prime Minister, He resigned his Senate seat and won the House of Representatives vacancy caused by Holt's death. But for most of the period of the by-election, Gorton was Prime Minister but not a member of the Parliament. There is no specific constitutional requirement that the Prime Minister should be a Member of the House of Representatives, rather than the Senate, but this 'convention' has always been followed in Australia. This contrasts with the British situation where, until the middle of the 19th century, most Prime Ministers were members of the House of Lords, not the Commons. In this century, though, the convention in Britain also has been that the Prime Minister should sit in the lower House, a convention which led several leading political figures in Britain who were entitled to sit as peers in the House of Lords, to have their hereditary positions set aside to enable them to seek election to the House of Commons so as to have a chance of becoming Prime Minister. In Australia the convention gained added force from Gorton's move, and subsequently several leading politicians, both Liberal and Labor, have tried to move from the Senate to the House in the hope of furthering their political ambitions. The convention means that the most important ministries, and the most powerful of a party's leaders, will be members of the House of Representatives rather than the Senate.

Since 1970, Federal Governments have usually contained about 27 Ministers, at least 20 of whom have always come from the House of Representatives. About half the Ministers are members of the Cabinet, which the is main decision-making body of the Government, and normally only one or two would be Senators. The result is that a larger proportion of Government Members in the House of Representatives are Ministers than is the case with the Senate and the Members of the House in the Ministry usually occupy the most important positions in the Government.

The same concentration of the top political leaders occurs on the Opposition side of the House of Representatives where the main 'shadow' Ministers sit. And one of the results of this concentration of political leadership in the House of Representatives is the concentration by the House generally on the political contest between Government and Opposition. As was mentioned in the first chapter, this is where the political theatre is situated. It is in the House of Representatives that the major battles over the policies of Government are fought out. This is where the Prime Minister and the Leader of the Opposition are face to face, battling for the best headlines and the best reports in the media and out among the voters. It is in the House that most important Government announcements are made by the Prime Minister and his Ministers, and where the Opposition will launch its main attacks against the Government.

For constitutional reasons, all financial legislation is introduced into the House and not the Senate, and this makes it imperative that the Treasurer is a member of the lower House. It also means that the annual Budget is presented first to the House of Representatives (though the Senate has developed a way of getting a look at it at the same time as the House). Because most Ministers are members of the House, most of the Bills are introduced in the House rather than the Senate. The Government and the Opposition spell out their main ideas about each piece of legislation during the debates in the House of Representatives, but they only

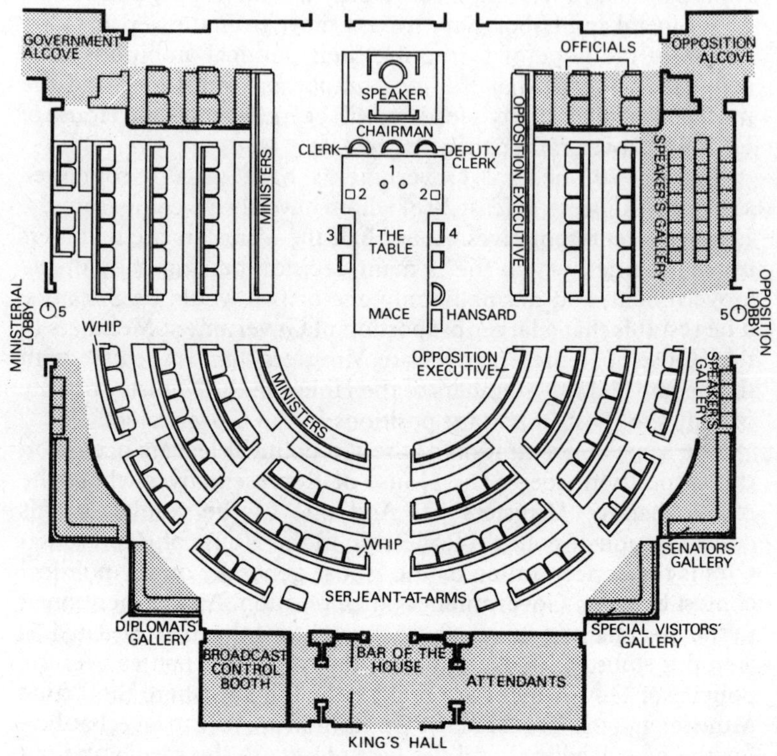

1. Sand-glasses
2. Despatch Boxes
3. Prime Minister or Minister in charge
4. Leader of the Opposition or Member
   of the Opposition Executive
5. Timing clocks (above lobby)

Note: Area not shaded grey defined as
'area within the seats alloted to Members'

The House of Representatives Chamber

rarely go through any Bill on a word-by-word basis—that detailed consideration is left to the Senate.

The Senate

The Senate is the 'upper' House and occasionally is referred to as the 'States' House'. This refers to the real reason for its creation—to protect the interests of the smaller States. But it has only rarely acted directly to protect the States, because of the way political parties dominate the workings of the Senate. A Senator is mostly elected because he has the backing of a particular political party, not because he claims to represent the whole interests of his State in some non-political way. But in theory the Senate is there to represent State interests. Each of the six States is represented by twelve Senators, and each of the two Territories by two Senators.

The results in a Senate election (whether held at the same time as the House of Representatives election or not) make no difference to the selection of the Government (though some of those elected for the Senate will no doubt win places in the new Government). Under the latest electoral system used in the Senate, it would be most unusual for any Government to have a majority in the Senate. The system seems likely to result most of the time in both the Labor Party and the Liberal–National Party coalition having less than half the members of the Senate, with the Australian Democrats, and smaller groups or parties such as those of Senator Harradine from Tasmania, holding the remaining places. This means that the smaller parties hold the 'balance of power'. In any conflict between the Government and the Opposition, it is these smaller parties which will decide the outcome.

One of the accepted roles for 'upper Houses' is to give more detailed consideration to proposed legislation than is possible in the House of Representatives. By the time most legislation is considered by the Senate, the main parties have already made clear their political attitudes towards it during debate in the House of Representatives. Rather than simply repeating everything that was said in the House, the Senators tend to concentrate on the detail of the legislation, to make sure it really carries out what it is intended to do. Much of this work is done by the Senate sitting as a committee, and considering a Bill on a clause-by-clause basis. The result is that because the Senate's consideration of proposed laws is less hurried and less harried, and out of the political spotlight, it is often able to remove errors which have crept into the draft of the

Bill. The very fact that the Bill has to go through two Houses of the Parliament, also means that the Government has a chance to have second thoughts about its proposals before they finally become law.

For a long time, the Senate has taken on a supervisory role over subordinate legislation. These are the regulations and ordinances which spell out the details of the laws passed by the Parliament. They are approved by the Governor-General but are subject to review by either House of Parliament. The Senate has a small committee which examines every piece of subordinate legislation, and measures it against a series of guidelines to ensure that it does not, for example, interfere with personal liberties, or give too much power to Ministers. The Senate does not have the power to amend these regulations, but it has become accustomed to using a threat that it will reject any which it thinks should be changed to persuade the Government to make the alterations it thinks necessary.

Since the 1970s one of the most distinctive functions the Senate has taken upon itself has been its committee work. Although the House of Representatives also has a range of committees, they do not cover anywhere near the amount of work undertaken by the Senate committees. The Senate has a series of committees which are arranged so as to cover the whole range of Government. At any one time, they are each likely to be examining dozens of policy issues. In addition the Senate has committees to examine in minute detail the estimates of Government expenditure which are presented with the annual Budget. It also establishes committees to undertake major investigations on particular problems.

The Senate has not taken on any activities in line with its supposed role as a 'States' House'. On a few occasions in the past, Senators have voted against their party in order to protect what they considered to be a more important interest of their home State. However it has been argued that Senators perform this role within their parties rather than in the Senate itself. The fact that all States have the same number of Senators means that the smaller States have a bigger representation in the parliamentary parties than they would otherwise have—particularly as the proportional representation system used in the Senate means that each major party does get some Senators elected in each State. At times, Tasmania has been represented in the House of Representatives by just one party—for example in the 1960s, Labor won each of the five House of Representatives seats from Tasmania, while in the late 1970s and 1980s, the Liberals won all five seats. The Senate system ensured that Tasmania did have something of a voice in the Liberal and Labor party rooms in the Parliament irrespective of the results in the House of Representatives elections.

Disputes between the House and the Senate

The parliamentary system of government does not necessarily require that there should be two Houses of the Parliament. Queensland has operated with a single House of Parliament for more than half a century. New Zealand has only a one-House parliament, and so does Papua New Guinea, which in most other respects copied its parliamentary and governmental system from Australia. However, the two-House system is the usual system adopted in federations such as the United States, Canada and India, where it is felt some special protection is necessary for distant or disadvantaged districts or States, or where the smaller units require some special guarantees to persuade them to join the federation (as occurred in Australia).

Where there are two Houses of Parliament, however, there is no general rule about how powerful each of them should be. In the United States the Senate is the more powerful part of the Congress because of a special role it is given in approving Cabinet and judicial appointments and treaties. But in most British parliamentary systems the lower House is the more powerful. In Britain itself, the House of Lords has had considerably fewer powers than the House of Commons since 1911. The House of Lords cannot reject a Budget or other financial legislation which has been approved by the House of Commons, and with most other proposed laws it can only delay but not defeat them.

In Australia the two Houses are almost equal (some of the differences and their significance are examined in Chapter 10). Most importantly, there are no limitations on the power of the Senate to reject proposed laws passed by the House of Representatives. This applies as much to the Budget and other financial and tax laws as to any other proposals. To some extent this gives the Senate the power to limit the life of a Government, by refusing to pass its Budget or give it 'supply'.[2]

---

[2] 'Supply' is parliamentary approval for the Government to spend money on public service salaries and other Government administrative and policy activities. The term is often used to include all financial approvals needed by the Government, though in fact most of the Government's finances are approved in the annual Budget, and the supply Bills are passed to provide it with finance between the end of the financial year and the time when the Budget is passed about five months after the new financial year begins.

It was the Senate's threat to use this power in 1974 and 1975 which resulted in a double dissolution of the Parliament on the first occasion, and dismissal of the Government by the Governor-General, together with a double dissolution, on the second. It is the fact that the Senate has such strong powers, and the fact that in recent times the political party or parties which are in the majority in the House of Representatives do not at the same time have a majority in the Senate, which results so frequently in the two Houses being brought into such serious conflict. There is no easy way for the conflict to be settled. Normally, either one House or the other has to give way. But the Constitution provides another solution through its provisions for a double dissolution. If the Senate has on two separate occasions, at least three months apart, rejected a law proposed by the House of Representatives, the Government can get the Governor-General to call an election for the House of Representatives and the whole of the Senate. If the Government is re-elected in the House but still does not have a majority in the Senate, it can have a joint meeting of the two Houses to pass the contested laws. But the procedure involved is obviously time-consuming (at least five months from the first refusal by the Senate to pass the proposed law) and very risky for the Government, which may simply lose the election. And after the double dissolution, it may still not control the Senate. Most of the time the Government simply has to be prepared to compromise with its opponents in the Senate, while both sides try to persuade the people who elected them that they are acting in their best interests.

CHAPTER 3

The Parliament's Timetable

The Government would grind to a halt if all the members of the Parliament, including Ministers, were required to be present in the House or the Senate every moment that the Parliament was sitting. So Parliament, and the Government, have evolved a series of devices to ensure that Parliament and Government can both at the same time pursue their separate tasks, while Ministers remain on hand to contribute when necessary to the proceedings of Parliament and to answering, explaining and accounting to Parliament for their ministerial activities.

The simplest but most important device available to them is the parliamentary timetable. Many parliamentary activities are entirely predictable or occur at times which can be determined in advance. Other parliamentary activities can be set down for particular times and the members of the Parliament, Ministers and backbenchers alike, can thus plan their activities with some certainty.

But these timetables are not immutable. On a day-by-day basis, and even a minute-by-minute basis, either the Government or the Opposition can try to spring a surprise on the other side. And what at one time might be a regular program of sitting can be changed under pressures of time and political circumstances. For decades, the Parliament sat on just three days a week. In recent years, however, it has been sitting four days a week, but for fewer weeks, and on a yearly basis, for fewer days. For many years the Budget has been introduced in August, a month and a half after the beginning of the financial year: almost everyone acknowledges that it would be better for a Budget (which is meant to be a planning document covering the whole financial year) to be introduced before the financial year begins on 1 July, and eventually a Government can be expected to try such an experiment. Changes, however, upset routine arrangements, and both backbenchers and Governments need to be convinced that changes in the parliamentary timetable will bring them positive benefits.

The parliamentary year

Parliament meets in two groups of sitting periods each year—from February through to May or June, and from mid-August through to November or December. In recent years it has met for approximately two weeks in every four during those periods, and for four days in each of those sitting weeks. Elections inevitably reduce the time available for parliamentary sittings. The busiest parliamentary year for a Government which lasts its full three years tends to be the middle year of its term.

The sittings beginning in February are referred to as the Autumn sittings; those starting in August are the Budget sittings. The Budget and its associated legislation completely dominate the August to November sittings. The Budget is introduced on the first night of the August sitting, and it generally does not pass through its full parliamentary process until mid-November. The House of Representatives spends up to three weeks in a general debate on the Budget's provisions, and several weeks in detailed discussion of its departmental estimates. The Senate undertakes a similar process, though its estimates consideration is far more detailed than that of the House and it takes place in small committees, where Ministers and departmental officials are questioned minutely about their proposals and their previous spending habits.

The Autumn sittings do not have any such marked focus. Because elections are generally held in November–December, or February–March, the first session of the new Parliament is normally in autumn. The session begins with an address by the Governor-General which officially opens the new Parliament and which puts the Government's objectives on the parliamentary record. The Government's policies are then debated at some length in what is called the 'address-in-reply' to the Governor-General's speech. This normally lasts a few weeks and provides the opportunity for members to discuss almost any subject in which they might be interested. It also gives the Government the chance to begin introducing the legislation which it considers to be important and which has completed the drafting process. Not all the Bills introduced in this session will be completed during the sittings. Some of the more important ones may be held over to allow public debate and negotiations with interested groups. They often will be taken up early in the following sittings, while the Opposition is digesting and determining its attitude to new legislation then being introduced.

For many years Parliament sat only on Tuesdays, Wednesdays and Thursdays, for three weeks in a row, and then took a fortnight's break. This arrangement had the advantage of allowing MPs and Senators from places quite distant from Canberra to leave their offices and homes on Monday and return to them on Friday, spending their weekends in their electorates and at home and with their families. In the early 1970s the Parliament experimented briefly with a sitting period designed to reduce travel back to the electorate: a sitting would last from Tuesday to Friday and then from Monday to Thursday in the succeeding week, the idea being that MPs and Senators from more distant States would spend the weekend between the two sitting weeks in Canberra. But it simply did not work that way—all but a very few parliamentarians still tried to get home each weekend. However, the arrangement was revived under the Hawke Government, along with a re-arrangement of the Parliament's workload during the week. The aim in part was to reduce work pressures on Ministers and MPs, following an outbreak of serious illness among MPs which seemed to be associated with the way Parliament was being conducted.

The Parliamentary day

Parliamentary sitting times have to accommodate one major non-parliamentary occasion—the time set aside for the major political parties to have their separate meetings of their parliamentary members. This used to occur on Wednesday mornings, but since the sitting times have been re-arranged, the party meetings are now set down for Tuesday mornings.

The new timetable for sittings of the House of Representatives is:

	FIRST WEEK	SECOND WEEK
Monday	—	2 p.m.–6.30 p.m. 8 p.m.–11 p.m.
Tuesday	2 p.m.–6.30 p.m. 8 p.m.–11 p.m.	2 p.m.–6.30 p.m. 8 p.m.–11 p.m.
Wednesday	10 a.m.–12.45 p.m. 2 p.m.–8 p.m.	10 a.m.–12.45 p.m. 2 p.m.–8 p.m.
Thursday	10 a.m.–6.30 p.m. 8 p.m.–11 p.m.	10 a.m.–6.30 p.m. 8 p.m.–11 p.m.
Friday	10 a.m.–12.45 p.m. 2 p.m.–4.30 p.m.	—

The time the House actually finishes is likely to vary according to the amount of business the Government wishes to conclude. Every set of sittings concludes with a series of late nights (or more accurately, early mornings).

The Senate's sitting times are very similar, though it meets at 9 a.m. on Fridays and tries to conclude at about 6.30 p.m. on the Thursday in the second sitting week.

One feature of the new system is that Question Time, which used to be the first major item of business for the Parliament on any sitting day, no matter what time the sitting began, is now held at a fixed time, 2 p.m. Another is that the Parliament no longer inevitably sits late at night—by shortening some of the meal breaks, the timetable allows a 7 p.m. finish to the parliamentary day at least once a week, instead of what used to be the standard finishing time of 11 p.m. or even later.

The standard order of business in the House of Representatives on Mondays and Tuesdays is for Questions without notice at 2 p.m., to be followed after about 45 minutes by the presentation of papers by Ministers, statements by Ministers, the presentation of petitions, any Matter of Public Importance (MPI) (this is usually at the choice of the Opposition), and finally, for most of the day, Government business, which is usually the discussion of Government legislation but which includes, for example, the address-in-reply debate mentioned earlier.

On Wednesdays, Thursdays and Fridays, the mornings begin with Government business (though on Thursday for several hours the House has a grievance debate or a general business debate). Questions come on at 2 p.m., to be followed again by the presentation of papers, ministerial statements and petitions, and any discussion of a Matter of Public Importance, before Government business is once again resumed. On each day of the week, an adjournment debate is scheduled to begin 45 minutes before the House concludes for the day.

The major differences with the Senate's program is that it normally allows an hour for questions, it sets aside an hour each week for the discussion of parliamentary committee reports, and it provides more time for discussion of MPIs and general business.

Both the House and the Senate produce two documents indicating the business before Members or Senators on each sitting day. The formal *Notice Paper* lists all the items of Government and general business which the House or Senate has on its agenda, in the order they are intended (for the moment) to be dealt with. However, the list under Government business can contain scores of items, ranging from Bills which have been

..THESE END-OF-SESSION SITTINGS ARE MURDER...

introduced and only partly debated, to motions to take note of various ministerial statements or reports (which may or may not ever be debated). On most days the two Chambers will only deal with the first few items on this list. But the *Notice Paper*, more importantly, also lists questions which have been placed on notice by Members or Senators, and the date on which questions were asked. The *Notice Paper* thus provides a constant reminder of what questions have not been answered, and the length of time they have remained unanswered. Occasionally a Minister's failure to answer questions will prompt further questions and/or complaints.

The Member or Senator wanting to know what his Chamber will be doing on a particular day will turn not to the *Notice Paper* but to an 'informal' document setting out the expected daily program. The program will indicate only those items of government or general business which are expected to be dealt with on the day in question. The House of Representatives program tries to indicate the time any proposed ministerial statements will be made. However, it provides no real guide to what will occur in the Chamber if the Opposition decides for political reasons to disrupt proceedings in any serious way.

Petitions

Petitions are one of the oldest forms of parliamentary activity, dating back to the 13th century. In their modern form they allow members of the public to communicate directly to the Parliament, o tell the Parliament of a particular problem and to seek Parliamentary action to remedy it. These days they tend to be concerned with a current political problem, and their aim is to persuade MPs, Senators or the Government or Opposition, that they should pay attention to the particular views put forward in the petition. Petitions can be signed and presented by just one person, or by hundreds of thousands of people—the larger the number of signatures, the greater the political impact. However, size alone is not the necessary determinant of the reaction which will result. In 1963 an MP presented a petition from the Aboriginal people of Yirrkala asking for the appointment of a Parliamentary committee to inquire into an intended resumption of land from an Aboriginal reserve. The petition was pasted on a bark sheet which was carved and decorated. Its unusual nature attracted public attention which of course was what was intended. The House agreed to the formation of the Committee which was requested. Petitions may also serve to arouse public interest in a particular subject. In the late

1960s a massive petition circulated in Western Australia seeking the abolition of death duties. The petition aroused public awareness to such an extent that its originator was able to win election to the Senate as an independent, and death duties were gradually abolished by the States and the Commonwealth.

A petition may be presented either to the House of Representatives or the Senate, but the person organising the petition must decide the petition's destination before he begins to collect signatures. This is because the petition has to conform to a set style. It has to be addressed either 'To the Honorable the President and Members of the Senate in Parliament assembled', or to 'The Honourable the Speaker and Members of the House of Representatives in Parliament assembled'. A petition to the House of Representatives then takes the form: 'The humble petition of certain citizens of Australia [or electors] respectfully showeth [and then states the circumstances]. Your petitioners therefore humbly pray that [terms of the action sought]. And your petitioners, as in duty bound, will ever pray'. This is then followed by the signatures of the petitioners. The words used in a Senate petition are slightly different but follow the same general style. Petitioners have to be presented by an MP or Senator and they first have to be checked by the Clerk to ensure that they are in the proper form. It is not necessary for the MP or Senator to agree with the terms of the petition.

Until 1970, petitions were not widely used in the Commonwealth Parliament. Between 1901 and 1969 the House received an average of 72 petitions a year—about one for each day it sat. The Senate received far fewer, and in many years received only one or two throughout the whole year. Through the decade of the 1970s, however, the House received an average of almost 1500 a year, and the Senate somewhat less. This influx caused both Houses to change the way in which they dealt with petitions. Originally a Senator or Member made a formal presentation of the petition, and its terms were then read out in full. But gradually the procedures have been shortened so that when similar petitions are presented, only the general terms of one of them are read, the full petitions being recorded in *Hansard*. Because of concern that the petitions were not receiving sufficient attention, the House of Representatives has decided that relevant ministers should be officially informed of any petitions directly affecting their administration.

Petitions blossomed in 1970 because political parties, interest groups and individuals realised that the presentation of a petition was a guaranteed way of getting a particular point of view on a political subject mentioned in the national Parliament. People are not restricted in the number of petitions they can organise or sign or have presented to the Parliament, and although the Parliament does not spend as much time as it did in airing the subject of individual petitions, it does provide something of a forum for anyone who goes to the trouble of arranging for a petition.

Notices

A notice of motion is the formal way in which any MP or Senator signifies that he wants to put a proposal to Parliament. But like the petition, its form has also come to be used to make a particular political statement, rather than as part of the process for which it was intended. And as with the petition, the Parliament has had to modify its procedures to ensure that its time was not swamped with material which was not directly connected with its normal work.

In neither House is an ordinary Member of Senator simply allowed to stand on his feet and propose a motion or begin a debate. There are laid down in the Standing Orders of both Houses certain procedures which must be followed in order to initiate any discussion. One of those procedures is the giving of notice, and the Houses have provided particular times at which MPs and Senators can stand and announce their intentions to move particular motions at some future time. However, because time is limited, most of the notices of motion are never reached and never debated.

In the 1980s, however, MPs began using the device of giving a notice of motion to make the kind of political statement which was also being made through petitions. The MP or Senator was able to deal with topics of immediate interest, and to spell out the reasons for his opposition, say, to a new decision announced by the Government, or to comment on some particular political development in such a way as to attack political opponents. The tactic was used particularly on days when the proceedings of the particular Chamber were being broadcast, and the result was that a listener would hear a series of proposed notices of motion condemning particular policies to which there could be no reply. Eventually, however, the House of Representatives changed its rules to prevent this from happening because dozens and sometimes scores of motions were being read out. MPs can still give notice of motions, but they do so in writing. The notices from the House of Representatives are no longer broadcast to a public which would not appreciate that the Parliament was not going to debate or decide any of the matters being put forward.

Question Time

Question Time is the normal highlight of the parliamentary day. It is the time when the Parliament is best attended by its members and the time when political confrontation is most apparent. It is at Question Time that Ministers have to account directly to Parliament for their Ministerial activities, answering questions of which they have no notice. Ministers also receive questions of which they do have notice, normally about matters requiring detailed investigations by their departments, or detailed information. Questions on notice are asked and answered in writing. They are recorded in the formal notice paper when they are asked and in *Hansard* when they are answered.

The Commonwealth Parliament has evolved its own unique form of Question Time. Question Time in the House of Representatives lasts about 45 minutes, and in the Senate about an hour. During those times any Minister may be asked a question seeking information, or pressing for action. Generally, however, questions overtly try to make political points. The Speaker first calls on a questioner from the Opposition, and when that question is answered, calls on a question from the Government backbenches. Questions continue to alternate between Opposition and Government throughout Question Time. When the Opposition is called on, the Leader of the Opposition and the Deputy Leader have precedence over all other Opposition members (in the Senate, precedence is given just to the Opposition Leader). The Speaker or President tries to choose other questioners in such a way as to share questions among members or Senators evenly.

Opposition members try to ask questions which will embarrass the Government in relation to policies or ministerial performances. Government questioners try to redress the balance by asking questions which highlight praiseworthy aspects of Government policy, or which allow Ministers to try to denigrate Opposition policies. There are limits imposed by the standing orders on the type of questions which can be asked and the way in which they can be asked, though the Speaker and President tend to be fairly flexible in their application of the rules because of the highly political function which Question Time serves. Questioners must ask questions, rather than make their own short speeches. The standing orders say that questions should not contain arguments, inferences, imputations, epithets, ironical expressions or hypothetical matter and may not ask for an expression of opinion or for a legal opinion. But questioners never seem to have any trouble in expressing their questions in such a way as to make their own views clear, or to demonstrate their antagonism towards the policies or decisions of their political opponents.

Although questions may be asked of any Minister, a particular Minister may decline to answer a question, or to pass it on to some more appropriate Minister for an answer. Questions which are directed to the Prime Minister are often answered by another Minister who is directly responsible for the administration of policy in relation to the subject-matter of the question.

When Ministers do answer questions they have few limitations placed on them. Their answers must be relevant to the questions asked, but there is no formal time limit on answers, and it is not difficult for a Minister to make almost any answer relevant. The result is that Ministers who are adept at the use of Question Time are able to use questions to attack their opponents or praise their own policies, irrespective of whether the questions originate from their own side or from the Opposition. Ministers sometimes ask Government backbenchers to ask them a particular question so that they can give a well-rehearsed answer to the Parliament. Such questions are sometimes called 'Dorothy Dixers'. But Ministers are also able to anticipate most of the questions which will be put to them by Opposition members, and spend some time preparing themselves to answer any matters of current political concern in their areas of responsibility. It is only rarely that an Opposition question finds a Minister completely unprepared, and it is even more rare that a Minister who has not anticipated a particular question is unable to deal satisfactorily with it.

Ministers receive most of the questions asked during Question Time, but questions may also be asked of the Speaker, other officers of the House, and even backbenchers, but only concerning matters connected with the business of the House, of which the member has charge (such as a committee). Such questions are rarely asked, and even more rarely are attempted questions held to be in order.

Question Time comes to an end whenever the Prime Minister or Minister in charge of the House or Senate asks that further questions be put on notice. This is a signal that further questions will not be answered by Ministers, even if they are asked.

There is no limit to the number of questions which MPs and Senators can put on notice seeking information from Ministers, even though occasionally departments complain at the amount of time and effort required to provide full answers to some questions. Questions on notice do serve a very real purpose of providing information for the Opposition in particular, and several thousand such questions are asked each year, three or four times as many as are asked without notice.

Seeking information has ceased to be a real function of questions without notice. Almost all questions are asked for overtly political reasons and almost all answers seek to score points rather than provide information—unless the giving of information is itself a political exercise. Question Time provides an opportunity for the Government and the Opposition to confront one another and for several dozen backbenchers and Ministers to expose their political skills on what are generally the most important or sensitive political subjects of the day. There is no other activity of the Parliament which provides the same tense atmosphere or air of political excitement, though Question Time can sometimes turn out to be dull and uninteresting if the Opposition has few shots to fire, and the Government is preoccupied with other events.

Matter of Public Importance (MPI)

Almost every sitting day the Opposition is given an opportunity to have a Parliamentary debate on a subject of its own choosing. This is partly to compensate it for the fact that most of the Parliament's time is spent debating government business—mainly the Government's proposed legislation. The procedures used to allow the Opposition debate have varied over the years, but the latest system in use in the Parliament is that the Opposition proposes a debate on a Matter of Public Importance (MPI), a debate which is held shortly after Question Time, and which is limited to three speakers a side in the House of Representatives, or to a maximum of two hours in the Senate. The Opposition is required to notify the Government two hours before the proposed debate of the subject (to allow the appropriate Minister and any backbenchers a chance to prepare their material). The MPI is usually phrased in such a way as to express some condemnation of a particular Government policy or action, or a view about some political or economic development—for example, early in 1985 there were MPIs in the House of Representatives on 'The failure of the Government to act in accordance with the national interest in respect of ANZUS and ASEAN', and, 'The damage already done to the cause of genuine tax reform by the factionalism within the Government'. Theoretically, MPIs can also be advanced by members of the Government, and the presiding officer is then required to choose which of the proposed discussions raises the more important issues. However, the Government normally does not interfere with the Opposition's choice of the subject for debate. If the Opposition introduces a censure motion, the MPI for the day is generally abandoned—the Opposition having used its time for a debate and decided on its subject.

The MPI debate ends automatically after two hours, or when the agreed (between the two sides) number of speakers have finished, or when the Minister in charge moves for the 'business of the day' to be called on. A significant feature of the MPI is that no vote is taken when the debate ends.

Ministerial statements

A ministerial statement gives the Government a chance to set the political agenda which is before the Parliament. A ministerial statement generally concerns a matter of significant Government policy, or details the results of particular actions by a Minister— for example, the results of an overseas visit by a Prime Minister. Ministerial statements are normally on subjects which do not need to be implemented by legislation, and this is particularly the case in foreign affairs and defence matters. When a Minister is to make such a statement, he gives a copy of it, in confidence, to the Opposition shadow Minister two hours before the statement is due to be made to the Parliament, so that the Opposition has a chance to make an immediate response to it. Parliament used to provide a considerable amount of time for general debates on ministerial statements, but this has largely ceased in the House of Representatives, and the Opposition has to respond immediately or not at all. Statements used to be made so as to catch the maximum listening audience on the parliamentary broadcast (in late afternoon) but now are given so as to allow the Minister time to hold a press conference after his statement has been made, so that it will be carried on television news bulletins.

Presentation of papers

The Parliament expects or requires many bodies to report to it on their activities. It receives reports from its own committees, from ministerial Departments and from bodies which it has created by Statute. Some of these bodies are required to report because they receive financial grants from the Parliament, others because the Parliament created them so that it could be informed by them of particular activities. The presentation of such reports is an exercise in demonstrating the accountability of the Government or executive to the Parliament and it is part of the information process by which the Parliament is informed of matters it considers important. Literally hundreds of reports occupying tens of thousands of pages are tabled in the Parliament each year.

The tabling of a report by a Minister, or the Speaker, provides another opportunity for the launching of a debate. A motion 'that the report be printed' allows the contents of the report to be debated, though in the House, finding time for the debate may not be easy. The Senate, however, specifically sets aside a set time each week in which reports may be discussed.

Government business

Most of the Parliament's time (between 55 and 65 per cent) is devoted to Government business, and the main form of Government business is Government legislation. The Parliament considers between 200 and 250 pieces of legislation each year, debating some of them (the Bills associated with the Budget) for many weeks. Major Bills might be debated in the House over two or three days, but the time left for the average Bill is only an hour or so—time for the Minister to make his introductory speech, for the Opposition to indicate its attitude, and for perhaps one or two backbenchers only to speak. In fact, consideration of proposed legislation is not quite as skimpy as that analysis might suggest. Many Bills are debated together and are introduced to implement one particular policy. Often an amendment to an existing policy in relation, say, to the wool industry, will require the Parliament to pass four or five Bills, because the Constitution requires the separation of taxes or money-collecting laws from other laws, and the making of grants for the implementation of policies also requires a profusion of legislation (see Chapter 10). Backbenchers are able to speak on most legislation which interests them. But what has happened over the years is that the time permitted for each speech has been limited and reduced (it is now 20 minutes) so as to allow maximum participation in debate.

Towards the end of the Autumn or Budget sittings, the Parliament usually finds that it has a great deal more legislation to pass than it can possibly manage if it keeps to its regular timetable. This occurs in part because legislation may have been introduced fairly late in the sittings. The amount of time available to discuss each Bill is greatly reduced, and occasionally Governments have to resort to either 'gagging' debates or introducing a 'guillotine'.

The first simply involves cutting off a particular debate, while the second sets a limited timetable during which a series of Bills have to be debated and voted on.

General business

It is under this heading that private Members or Senators (members of the Opposition, or Government backbenchers) may introduce matters on which they want the House or Senate to vote—rather than merely debate. The proposals they put before the Parliament may be either simply motions, expressing a particular point of view, or seeking some Government action, or they may be in the form of a Bill, seeking to create some new law, or amend an existing law.

The amount of time provided for general business is comparatively small in the House of Representatives—an hour or so half a dozen times a year. The Senate, because of the strength of the voting position of the Opposition and minor parties, spends considerably more time on general business.

Private members' Bills are introduced fairly frequently, to highlight an Opposition (or minor party) policy, but they rarely get beyond the second reading stage in the House in which they are introduced. However, some important private members' Bills have been passed by the Parliament, and have become law. One such Bill, passed in 1924, is responsible for voting being compulsory at federal elections. Another, the Matrimonial Causes Act of 1955, was introduced by a Government backbencher, and resulted in later Government-sponsored legislation to introduce uniform divorce laws in Australia. Another settled the dispute between the Houses and between Parliament and the Government over the siting of the proposed new Parliament House.

Grievances

A 'grievance debate' is another formal method provided to allow backbenchers to discuss very briefly (in a 10-minute speech) any issue at all which concerns them. It may be a problem brought to them by an elector, who is having problems with part of the federal bureaucracy, or it may be an aspect of Government or Opposition policy which is discussed. The grievance debate alternates with general business motions to take up the time provided for general business.

Business of the Senate

In 1970 the Senate introduced a new procedure to ensure that motions concerning Senate committees can be readily considered by the Senate without intruding on the time allocated for general business. Business of the Senate takes precedence over Government or general business and is used to allow debate on any proposals for the creating of new committees, or for sending references for investigation by any committee, and for the presentation of reports from committees and the debating of those reports.

Adjournment

The motion at the end of the day to adjourn the House or the Senate provides yet another opportunity for backbenchers to raise any issue which concerns them. For a half to three-quarters of an hour on most sitting days, backbenchers may speak for 10 minutes about almost any subject which concerns them. If it is a matter concerning a particular Government department, the backbencher tells the responsible Minister of the subject he will be raising, so that the Minister can hear and respond to it quickly, either briefly intervening in the debate, or seeking a quick answer from his department the next day.

Some other procedures

The regular routine of the Parliament can be interrupted in many ways which are provided for in the standing orders of the two Houses. It is usual for all other business to be suspended when the Opposition gives notice of a censure motion. The censure is immediately moved and debated and a vote taken before the House resumes its ordinary business (though Question Time is normally abandoned for the day after a censure motion).

At any time a member can gain precedence by raising a matter of privilege, though a reference of a supposed breach of privilege to the privileges committee will not be debated immediately unless the Speaker is convinced that there is a prima-facie case of a breach.

Members can also take 'points of order' at almost any time, provided they can gain the Speaker's attention. A point of order is a claim that something has been said or done in the House contrary to the provisions of the Standing Orders. A decision by the Speaker is sometimes objected to and any member can move a motion of dissent from the Speaker's ruling. Such a motion is debated immediately and then voted on.

Members frequently complain that they have been 'misrepresented' either by something that has been said by another Member in the House, or by some report in the media concerning something they themselves have said or done. The Speaker normally allows such 'personal explanations' immediately after

Question Time (when most of the occasions of misrepresentation happen). Members are normally required simply to explain the way in which they have been misrepresented, and are not allowed to debate the rights and wrongs of the issue.

Another device used by the Opposition to raise an issue is to move suspension of the standing orders so as to allow a discussion on that issue. There is generally no expectation that the Standing Orders will be suspended. However, debate does take place on the motion for suspension in such a way as to allow the Opposition to state its particular complaint.

It is important for any MP or Senator to master the tricks of his particular House, and to try to adapt them to his own uses. But it is possible for MPs (and their critics) to get carried away with the intricacies of these procedures. While they are important in the running of the Parliament, they are only the means by which the Parliament is conducted. They are not its substance.

CHAPTER 4

The Key Players

In its political role, Parliament is dominated by the Prime Minister and his Ministers, and the Leader of the Opposition and his 'shadow' ministry. They all occupy special positions in the Parliament in a physical sense—sitting in the front benches on either side of the House of Representatives and the Senate (which explains the use of the word 'frontbencher' to describe those in leadership positions in the House and Senate, and 'backbencher' to describe those not holding any official position as MPs or Senators). The frontbenchers also have special privileges which recognise the importance of their roles in the parliamentary process.

The Prime Minister

The Prime Minister is the elected leader of the Government party (or Government coalition of parties) in the House of Representatives. Most of his time and energy are devoted to the general running of the Government, supervising the work of his ministry, and ensuring that so far as possible the Government is able to achieve its political objectives. One of those objectives is normally to try to keep the Government's popularity at a level which is sufficiently high to allow it to be successful at the next elections. The Prime Minister is also required to lead his Ministers and inspire his backbenchers by his performances in the House of Representatives. Prime Ministers who fail to do so are likely to find themselves troubled by rumours that they are going to be in difficulty holding on to their leadership, because Prime Ministers who do not perform well in the Parliament are generally being outperformed by the Opposition Leader. When that occurs, the Government's electoral prospects often begin to look dim.

When the Prime Minister is in the House of Representatives Chamber, he normally sits at a chair at the centre table, separated from his Ministers and his backbenchers. He invariably sits at the table, metaphorically at the head of his troops, during Question Time, and he also sits there when he is to take part in a debate. But when a Minister is making a significant policy announcement, or during an ordinary debate, the Prime Minister frequently retreats to sit on the frontbench.

Question Time is normally the most testing time in Parliament for a Prime Minister, but a time which most Prime Ministers appear to look forward to. There are more questions directed to the Prime Minister than to any other Minister, and the questions are normally not about the administration of particular policies but about current political controversies. The Prime Minister, for example, is likely to be questioned about the Government's standing in the public opinion polls (if they are low), relationships between the Government and an unco-operative state Government, the impact of international events on domestic policies, the work of a Royal Commission, and the apparent faults of his Ministers. He may, if he wishes, pass questions on to other Ministers if the questions concern their administration, and if he has sufficient confidence in their ability to answer. Questions requiring detailed replies, such as those on the economy or foreign affairs, he will normally refer to the appropriate Minister. However, the Prime Minister may have anticipated a particular question and may want to answer it himself because he has prepared an answer which he considers will make an impact on his own side, on the Opposition or, more importantly, on the Press Gallery journalists who sit through every Question Time. Occasionally the Prime Minister may wish to hand on a question to a Minister but the question has been phrased by the Opposition in such a way as to make it appear that he would be shirking a challenge if he did not answer it himself. But the Prime Minister has to be prepared to resist that challenge if he cannot produce an answer to satisfy his critics.

The Prime Minister during Question Time is always under pressure to perform well. His answers are more likely to be reported by the media than are the answers of other Ministers and, in any event, the way he performs will have more effect on the morale of his parliamentary colleagues (and sometimes of his opponents) than the actions of anyone else in the Parliament. In the long run, morale does matter, even if variations in the spirit of the major political parties are not instantly detectable by the average voter. For the same reason, the Prime Minister will normally be expected to lead the Government's debating response whenever it comes under serious Opposition attack, in the form of a censure motion or motion of no confidence in the Government.

But other than at Question Time, or during censure motions, or when important Government announcements are being made, the Prime Minister rarely appears in the House. He has virtually a permanent 'pair'[3] with the Leader of the Opposition, so that neither has to come into the House to record his vote on issues other than those which are generally regarded as being of special importance.

The Leader of the House

The Minister who is designated by the Prime Minister as Leader of the House occupies a vital role in parliamentary proceedings. He bears the ultimate responsibility for both strategy and tactics for the Government in the House of Representatives. He decides when legislation should be introduced, when it should be debated and for how long, and the timing of Government decisions and when they are announced in the House. He has to anticipate the moves which the Opposition might make to disrupt what for him is the orderly conduct of the Government's business through the House. The Opposition's viewpoint is quite different—it has to make its attitudes clear to the public in the best way it can, and often that will involve trying to frustrate the Government's legislative program. In the long run, the Government has the ability to force its legislation through the House because of its control of a majority of votes in the House. But there are innumerable ways for the Opposition to waste time and legitimately use provisions of the standing orders to upset the Government's timetable. One such method of time-wasting is to introduce a motion to suspend standing orders in order to move any other sort of motion at all which has nothing to do with what the Government wants to do. Each time an Opposition member

---

[3] A 'pair' is an arrangement between the Government and Opposition whips to allow a Member to be absent from a vote. In order to keep a fairly permanent balance between the two sides during any session of Parliament, the whips arrange that if a member from one side is to be absent from Parliament (through illness, for example, or because a Minister has to travel overseas on Government business) the other side tells one of its members not to vote during that absence. Pairs are normally arranged by the party whips and the arrangement is very convenient because there are always members from both sides who want or need to miss a sitting for some reason.

moves such a motion, up to half an hour can be wasted before the Government can get the House back to considering its business. There are many methods open to the Opposition which are not in the standing orders, such as creating such a racket that the Government is forced to move that an Opposition member be suspended from the House. And an Opposition can be quite creative in its disruption, to the extent of involving the Speaker in making rulings, and then moving dissent from his ruling. The fact that it is within the Opposition's power to make parliamentary life difficult for the Government is a powerful reason for the Government not to use its numbers too brutally, and it is the aim of the Leader of the House to make progress as much through co-operation with the Opposition as through the use of the force of its numbers.

But, in the last resort, the Leader can decide that a particular MP ought to be 'gagged' (this is done by passing a resolution that the member 'be no longer heard') or that a debate as a whole be gagged (by moving that the motion be put). Every vote takes precious time. When a division of the House is called, the bells are rung for two or three[4] minutes to call MPs from all over Parliament House, and then the votes have to be counted by marking names of each member off specially prepared lists, a process which takes six or seven minutes. When the Speaker or President orders the ringing of the bells to summon Members or Senators to a division or a quorum, bells are rung right through Parliament House, in all offices and in all the public places such as the refreshment rooms and the library (and even the toilets). The bells are mounted with red and green lights, and the appropriate light flashes when the bells are ringing to indicate whether it is the Senate (red) or the House of Representatives (green) which is calling its members to a division or quorum.

The Leader of the House has a series of options for dealing with such delays, apart from using the gag. One is simply to extend the time of each day's sitting, beyond its scheduled finishing time, until all the work he has set down on the program is completed, even if that means a 2 a.m. or 3 a.m. end to the parliamentary day. This tends to occur more towards the end of a sitting period, when

[4] The standard time for allowing members to reach the House when a division is called is two minutes, but the House of Representatives has occasionally adopted a three-minute period when alterations to the building have forced MPs to take accommodation far from the Chamber. In 1985 the House was using the three-minute period, the Senate two minutes. When two divisions are held in succession, the Speaker normally orders the bells to be rung for just one minute for the second, and subsequent, divisions.

the Government is anxious to ensure that all the legislation it has introduced is considered and passed by the Parliament before the recess. Late sittings are unpopular with all MPs and Senators, however, and the Leader of the House only resorts to them when it is absolutely necessary. When they do occur, the Opposition invariably complains that the Government is indulging in 'legislation by exhaustion'. Government backbenchers cannot complain publicly but they too disapprove of having to sacrifice their sleep. It is probably worse for Government backbenchers than for the Opposition. The Government has to keep its numbers available to pass the legislation; the Opposition can quietly tell many of its MPs to go home.

Late sittings always result in someone complaining about the Government's mismanagement of its parliamentary program, and that is always blamed on the Leader of the House.

Occasionally, the Leader of the House may have sufficient time available to him to allow the Opposition a fairly free rein, but this does not happen often, and when it does it displeases the Government's backbenchers. They do not like to see the Opposition winning any parliamentary victories. But unless the Leader of the House provides the Opposition with some latitude, he faces a constant battle with them and can never assume that what he wants the House to do, will in fact be done as he has planned.

The Leader of the House has to have clear goals and a sound knowledge of parliamentary tactics. He also has to be something of a diplomat in his negotiations with the Opposition, both inside the House and outside. (The negotiations inside the House take place literally behind the Speaker's chair, and generally relate to some change in previous arrangements about the order of business, or the provision of speaking time for some Minister or Opposition member.) He has to be continually on his guard and listening to what is happening in the Chamber, even when he is not in it, so that at a moment's notice he can hurry back in to take charge of the Government's response to whatever is happening.

The Leader of the House is responsible for the conduct of the whole of the Government's parliamentary business, but most of his time is taken with what is happening in the House of Representatives. In the Senate, another senior Minister is delegated as Manager of Government Business to look after the Government's interests in that Chamber. Because the Government normally does not control the Senate, the Manager of Government Business has a far more difficult and frustrating task than the Leader of the House. The Manager of Government Business has to negotiate with the Opposition and smaller parties about when particular issues will be debated, and the length of those debates. He simply does not have the numbers to force a gag of a debate unless he can persuade another party to support him. Much more compromise is necessary in the conduct of the Government's business in the Senate than in the House.

Ministers

The main responsibility of most other Ministers is simply to be present during Question Time and answer any questions concerning their area of ministerial responsibility. They have to prepare for this task quite carefully if they are not to be caught out by an Opposition question on a subject which they ought to know the answer to. The Minister is normally given a loose-leaf briefing book prepared by his Department which deals with every subject of current political interest, whether it is known to the public or not. The Department normally provides a suggested answer, which may provide a considerable amount of detail, or may advise the use of generalisations to fob off the questioner. The briefing book is usually supplemented by additional information from the Department shortly before Question Time, dealing with any subjects which may have been raised in the media since the last briefing note was prepared. And most Ministers hold a special briefing session with the more senior members of their personal staff immediately before Questions (some Ministers also have senior Departmental officers attend these briefings). These last-minute meetings will normally try to second-guess the questions which the Minister might receive, and suggest the way in which various problem areas should be handled.

Generally, the test of the Minister's political skill is the way he chooses to answer a particular question at a particular time. It may be appropriate on one day to provide a straight, informative answer, while on another it may be more appropriate to turn the answer into an attack on the Opposition or its policies. The circumstances (whether the Government is winning or losing the Question Time period, or whether it wants to push or avoid a particular subject) will dictate whether a Minister should answer a question as briefly as possible, or produce a long-winded boring response. There are no hard and fast rules, except that a Minister should scarcely ever be seen to be surprised by a particular question, or discomforted by it. The way a Minister handles Question Time will largely influence the way in which he is regarded by his colleagues, by his backbenchers and the Opposition, and by the Press Gallery. But because Question Time is normally limited to about 45 minutes in the House of Representatives, and each side only gets about eight questions, not every Minister has the same opportunity to demonstrate his skills. Popular topics will vary with the political climate, but questions to the Prime Minister and the Treasurer are clearly more frequent than questions to the Minister for Adminsitrative Services, or the Minister for Tourism. In fact, the Prime Minister tends to get about twice as many questions as the Treasurer, who in turn gets about twice as many as any other Minister. Trade, Primary Industry, Transport, Foreign Affairs, Defence and Health are the next most popular Ministers for questions, while those who tend to get the least are the Ministers for Science, the Capital Territory and Housing. A Minister may attract a certain proportion of questions simply because of the portfolio he holds (the Minister for Primary Industry is bound to get a large number of questions from members of the National Party, who represent rural electorates). But Ministers may also attract questions because of their lack of ability. A Minister who is seen to be inept will get more than his ordinary share of questions because it suits the Opposition to have Ministers showing at Question Time that they are not on top of their subjects (or that they do not give the public impression of being on top). Making a Minister look silly helps the Opposition persuade the public that the Government as a whole looks silly. In fact this does not happen very often, but when it does, the Minister is likely to be demoted or dropped altogether from the Ministry as soon as it can be arranged.

The other major responsibility for the Minister is the introduction of legislation for which he is responsible, and the making of any Ministerial statements on Government policy in his area. When introducing a Bill, the Minister makes a major speech explaining its contents and its purpose. He then sits through the debate on the Bill when it is resumed (normally a week after its introduction) and will normally reply to any major criticisms before the vote on the second reading of the Bill. In committee he will deal with any amendments which are suggested, replying to any questions which may be asked by the Opposition. If necessary he will be able to get assistance in answering any technical matters from members of his Department, sitting in special advisers' seats within the Chamber. A Minister is also responsible for seeing through the debate on any statement he has made, or paper which he has tabled.

Ministers also occasionally have to sit in the House when they are doing nothing at all. Although the Leader of the House is responsible for the running of the House, he, like other Ministers, cannot be expected to be in the Chamber the whole time, particularly as he also has a normal portfolio to administer. The Government therefore ensures that at least one Minister is in the House at all times, and this is done by the simple expedient of drawing up a roster on which all but the Prime Minister and the Treasurer are listed. Then, from the most junior to the most senior, Ministers are allocated one hour's duty in the House. The work is not arduous: it is simply a question of being there and holding the fort until the Leader of the House arrives if any difficulty arises. Leaving out times when all Ministers are present anyway, the duty roster keeps most Ministers in the House for an additional two or three hours a week. And the time is not wasted. Most Ministers take with them a bundle of correspondence which has to be signed, or departmental files which have to be read. For many, it is an opportunity to get away from the never-ending series of meetings they hold in their offices and elsewhere in Parliament House.

Ministers who sit in the Senate have a far more difficult time than do their colleagues in the House. Perhaps half a dozen Senate Ministers have to do the work that twenty or more do in the House. They have to represent House Ministers at Question Time, using the same briefs that have been prepared for the Minister in the House to answer what are often the same questions. Question Time in the Senate lasts an hour, and far more questions tend to be asked, because the Ministers give shorter answers. Also, because there are fewer people to ask questions, there is a greater possibility for questioners to ask supplementary (follow-up) questions and so a Senate Minister cannot so easily dismiss his questioner with a smart reply which does not directly give an answer. The Senate Ministers also have to present Bills on behalf of House of Representatives Ministers (which have usually already been passed by the House of Representatives) and steer them through all the processes of the Senate, including far more detailed committee investigation than they ever get in the House. This is additional to introducing their own Bills into the Senate. They also have to present the same ministerial statements to the Senate which have gone to the House of Representatives, and manage what could be longer debates. Given the number of Senate Ministers available (six or seven, as against twenty or so in the House), Senate Ministers have to spend three or four times as long on 'duty' in the Senate, but in circumstances which are far less easy. Most Ministers in the Senate face a situation where they simply cannot muster the numbers to control the events which take place there. They have to make arrangements with the

Opposition and with minor parties, and they have to do so from a position of weakness. They have to spend far more time negotiating than do Ministers in the House, and they can never be certain of the outcome until a vote is taken. And those who sit in the Cabinet have to mix their duties in the Senate Chamber with their duties as Cabinet Ministers, trying to attend their full range of meetings and discussions.

The Leader of the Opposition

The role of the Leader of the Opposition is far less clearly defined than is the Prime Minister's or his various Ministers. The Leader of the Opposition is assisted by an Opposition equivalent of the Leader of the House who determines moment-to-moment tactics, and who acts as the Opposition's liaison man with the Government's Leader of the House. Together they discuss when Bills should be debated, how many speakers there should be in any debate, and which ministerial statement of papers the Opposition wants to have time allocated to for debate. The Opposition's general strategy, however, is usually decided by the whole of its executive—the Opposition Leader plus the dozen or more people who are designated as 'shadow Ministers'. They generally meet the day before a two-week sitting begins, spending five or six hours working out the areas where they consider the Government is most vulnerable to attack, and generally deciding what issues should be pursued. The Opposition executive also discusses the legislation which is currently before the Parliament, and the attitude which the Opposition should take towards it. On each sitting day the Leader of the Opposition and his senior shadow Ministers and their advisers will discuss the particular tactics to be adopted on that day. They will make final decisions on which Matters of Public Importance should be debated (these having been determined in general terms by the fortnightly strategy meeting, and the subject of any concerted questioning which should be undertaken at Question Time. They also may decide occasionally that the whole of Question Time should be devoted to pursuing a particular subject of attacking a particular Minister. More rarely, they may even co-ordinate all the questions that the Opposition will ask, working out in what order they should be asked and by which Opposition MPs.

While there are Opposition spokesmen to 'shadow' each Minister, and be responsible for developing Opposition policy in that particular area, as well as keeping an eye on the way the

Minister is doing his job, the Opposition Leader's task is far more complex. In a sense he has to do what the Prime Minister does: provide leadership for all his MPs and Senators in the development of the party's policies and its political strategies. But unlike the Prime Minister he is expected to perform a great deal in the parliamentary arena. He has to lead the Opposition's fight in the House of Representatives on almost every contentious issue— unlike the Prime Minister he cannot leave issues to his main ministerial supporters. And if issues and politics are not breaking the Opposition's way, everyone expects him to find an issue that will work for the benefit of the Opposition, and to show the way it should be exploited in the Parliament.

He has to use the forums of the Parliament both to advance his own policies and to criticise those of the Government. But because of the way Parliament is organised, and because of the way the media reports what happens in Parliament, most of the Opposition Leader's efforts have to be devoted to attacking and trying to destroy the Government or its policies. It is easy for him to get a reputation as a person who is wholly destructive and never constructive and for him to be accused, in the best Australian tradition, of being a 'whinger'.

The Leader of the Opposition is expected to make major speeches in Parliament far more often than, say, the Prime Minister, and he has to speak on a vast range of subjects, including the economy, foreign affairs, and any other subject of current political significance or of prospective significance to the Opposition. But he is not tied down by the responsibilities of administering a Government Department, so he is able to spend much of his time preparing for the public side of his role. However, the Opposition Leader does have to spend almost as long as do Ministers seeing constituents and representatives of commmunity groups and pressure groups and VIPs. And he must make a special point of keeping in touch with backbenchers and the chairmen of the various party committees. He also sees many Australian and overseas diplomats—Heads of foreign embassies always seek to pay an official call on the Leader of the Opposition, and senior Australian diplomats make themselves available for discussions before they take up their postings, and on any return visits to Australia.

The Leader of the Opposition has a special responsibility during Question Time because both he and the Deputy Leader of the Opposition gain the Speaker's approval to ask a question whenever they wish. They have precedence over every other

Opposition member, and the result is that they ask several questions each day, while the average Opposition backbencher or shadow Minister has to wait for three weeks between questions. This precedence increases the pressure on the Opposition leaders to perform—otherwise their followers feel they are being deprived for no good reason of the opportunity of asking good questions and that the leaders are wasting their opportunities.

Above all, the Leader of the Opposition has to perform in such a way as to inspire his followers, both inside and outside the Parliament, and to provide them with the assurance that he can lead them to victory at the next elections. That involves consolidating the Opposition's forces and demonstrating the faults in the Government's policies and its personnel. The Parliament is not a very satisfactory medium for achieving those objectives—partly because of the Government's control over most of what happens in the House of Representatives. But it is the best forum that the Opposition has. If the Opposition Leader does not perform well inside the House of Representatives, his prospects for success in the wider electorate are not considered to be very high.

Another significant member of the Opposition is its Leader in the Senate. The balance of political parties in the Senate gives him a far more creative role than is available in the House of Representatives. The Senate Opposition Leader is normally in a position to bargain with the Government and minor parties about the way in which the Senate will conduct its business, the legislation it will devote its time to discussing, and the extent to which the Senate will debate general business, Opposition proposals, and committee reports. Because the Government is rarely in a position where it can successfully employ the 'gag', the Leader of the Opposition has the ability to hold up the Government's legislative program if he is not satisfied with arrangements made by the Government. He is also in a position to play an important political role, because with the help of minor parties, the Opposition can normally command enough votes to set up a Senate committee on any subject. The political and parliamentary effectiveness of the Opposition is greatly enhanced when the Government does not have a majority in the Senate and when there is close co-operation between the Leader of the Opposition and his Leader in the Senate.

CHAPTER 5

The Elected Officials

'Parliament' is a word with a long history. Four or five hundred years ago it meant a formal conference or council for the discussion of some matter or matters of general importance; a 'bout' of speaking; or a discussion or debate. At the same time it was being applied to the Great Council of England, which, together with the King, made the nation's laws. The word is derived from Old French, 'parlement', meaning simply 'speaking'. The modern parliament is still referred to as a debating forum, but this is a misleading description of its function, even though, on occasions, some great debates do occur in parliament.

But the Parliament of today is ill-equipped to stage those great debates, and there are very many factors which tend to prevent it from doing so. To begin with, the two 'sides' to the debate are not evenly balanced in terms of numbers. One side, the Government, has more members than the other, and it controls most of the matters which are discussed in the Parliament, and can alter the conditions and the length of the debate to suit its convenience. The majority side also chooses from among its own members the person who is to preside over the discussions and to enforce the rules. The presiding officer, while he tries to be fair to both sides, never resigns his membership of the majority side. The rules which he enforces (called the Standing Orders) are written in a way which deliberately favours the Government (the majority side).

It is only rarely that a rousing debate does occur in the Parliament, and then it seems it is almost in spite of the system. Occasionally there is an issue which is of such significance that it transcends the ordinary restrictions of the system. Traditionalists maintain that good debates were more common in the past, when Members had more time in which to speak, fewer subjects which had to be mastered, and made speeches which were intended directly to answer the arguments put forward by their opponents. For some decades, however, it has been the practice in the Commonwealth Parliament for Members to prepare speeches in advance and to read them formally, rather than orate them. One result is that although the speeches now are frequently better researched and contain more factual material, there is no sense of the debate ebbing and flowing. Members do often begin their speeches with a quick repudiation of what the previous speaker from the other side has said, but the main aim is to read what they themselves have prepared into the parliamentary record. When there is a freer debate, on a subject where there has been insufficient time for preparation, there is often resort to personal attack on the other side, rather than the discussion of the substance of an issue.

The proceedings of the Parliament are formally controlled by its elected Presiding Officers, the Speaker in the House of Representatives, and the President in the Senate. A Deputy Speaker and a Deputy President are also elected. The elections of these officers of the Parliament is the first task undertaken by each newly elected Parliament.

The Speaker

The title 'Speaker' has a long and distinguished history. The British House of Commons, from its earliest days in the 13th and 14th centuries, elected a 'speaker' to tell the King of its views and its resolutions. His role was a dangerous one. The messages which were given to the King did not always please him, and a number of Speakers died violent deaths, while others were imprisoned or expelled from office. When the King began choosing his Ministers from the Parliament, the Speaker was relegated to his modern role as the chief administrator of the Commons, as well as its presiding officer or chairman.

In England the Speaker does sit above party politics and enjoys very great prestige. The Speaker is elected from among the Members of Parliament, and normally from the party which is in Government at the time a vacancy occurs in the office of Speaker. But he is expected then to take a non-partisan attitude in his role as the Presiding Officer, and to divorce himself from party politics generally. This is made possible through the fact that he is not opposed for re-election to Parliament by the other party at election time, and he continues as Speaker even if there is a change of government. It is for him to decide when he will retire as Speaker. There is no political advantage gained by any party in having its man as Speaker, because the same privilege of not being opposed at election time is extended to the Speaker's three deputies, who are chosen so that each side has two of its members returned unopposed at each election. The Speaker lives in a set of apartments in the Palace of Westminster which contains the Houses of Parliament.

The Speaker of the House of Representatives occupies no such grand position. He is elected to Parliament as a party politician and he retains that role at all times, though he will try to be impartial in his rulings as chairman of the House. He is certain to be opposed by the other side of politics at the time of the next election, and if his side loses the election, he can be certain that he will cease to be Speaker. He can also expect that a great many of his rulings from the Chair will be challenged by the Opposition, and that these motions of dissent from the Speaker's ruling will mostly be decided by a party-line vote. This means he has no independent authority over the proceedings of the House, because if the Government disapproves of the way he is handling an issue, it too can move dissent, but its challenge will be successful in overruling him. Most Speakers do not attempt to cut themselves off from party politics. They attend the weekly meetings of their party, and sometimes committee meetings. Some make public partisan-political speeches, and not just at election time.

The Speaker is not expected at the time of his election to be a great expert on the procedures of the Parliament, though invariably he will have a good knowledge of them and will acquire considerable expertise through practice. But, initially at least, the Speaker is expected to rely on the advice given to him by the Clerk of the House, the permanent senior official of the House, who sits immediately to the front and to the right of the Speaker. He quickly turns or moves to the Speaker's side to advise him on procedures and the correct precedent to be followed on any necessary occasion.

When Sir Billy Snedden was Speaker, between 1976 and 1983, he undertook a deliberate campaign to try to improve the prestige and power of the Speaker in the House of Representatives. However, he was unable to persuade the major parties, or even a majority of backbenchers, that the idea of bringing in a non-partisan Speaker should be investigated. He conducted a poll of the 125 (as there then were) MPs asking them whether they supported a proposal for an all-party committee to investigate introducing the British tradition to the House of Representatives. Only 80 MPs replied, and only 47 were in favour.

Although he was unsuccessful in persuading his colleagues that the Speaker of the House should be above politics, he did help to persuade the Government to agree to a scheme sponsored by the Senate and developed by it over a 17-year period, to introduce budgetary and administrative changes which make the Speaker and the President of the Senate far more influential in the determination of the staffing of the bureacracies which provide necessary support for the functioning of the Parliament and its committees, and, even more importantly, in determining how much money should be allocated in the annual budget for the Parliament. Previously, the budget allocation for the parliamentary committees was decided by the Treasury or the Department of Finance and by the Cabinet, and there was no input at all from the Parliament itself, other than through consultations between the parliamentary departments and Treasury or Finance officials. This was changed to bring the Speaker and the President into the system, as representatives of the ordinary members of Parliament. They take the place which Ministers of ordinary Departments fulfil in the budgetary process, and are able to put their case before the Cabinet if necessary. The Presiding Officers also act in the manner of Ministers as the heads of the respective parliamentary departments of the House of Representatives and the Senate, and they share responsibility for the other parliamentary depart- ments—the Library, the Reporting service (*Hansard*), and the Joint House Department.

When he presides in the House, the Speaker is largely guided by the Standing Orders and by the precedents established by previous Speakers in the way he controls procedure and debate. His major problem is basically to keep order in the House. Question Time is often the most testing time for the Speaker. Both sides seek to make their political points, and the Speaker often has a difficult time keeping total control. He has to restrain excessive inter- jections, questions which do not meet the requirements of the Standing Orders, and answers which are too long and which cause too much reaction from the other side.

The Speaker is not expected to sit in control of the House for the whole of its sittings. He has the assistance of the Chairman of Committees, who acts as his deputy, and of a series of temporary deputies, who are selected by him. But the Speaker always takes the Chair at the formal beginning of each day's sittings (when he reads prayers), at the end during the adjournment debate, and during Question Time and other times when there is likely to be conflict in the House, or when there are important debates or proceedings.

The President

Until the 1970s the President of the Senate stood above the Speaker in the official table of precedence for the Commonwealth, immediately below the Governor-General and the Prime Minister. The Whitlam Government, however, decided that because the two Houses of Parliament were of equal standing, if not equal power, it was wrong to make the President more important that the Speaker who presided in the House where the Government was determined. A wrangle over precedence was solved with a neat compromise—the two presiding officers were given equal status, precedence being taken by the one who was first elected to his post. Nevertheless, there remain some official functions which make the President the more prestigious official, and require him to have a suite of rooms which are more opulent than those of the Speaker. In particular it is the President who plays host to the Governor-General or the Queen at the opening of Parliament or on official parliamentary occasions.

The role and position of the President have been made somewhat different from those of the Speaker by the nature of political representation in the Senate. Unlike the situation in the House of Representatives the Government does not invariably or inevitably control a majority in the Senate, so that it cannot ever be sure that its nominee will be elected as President. Even when it has a bare majority, a party cannot be absolutely guaranteed of success, because voting is by secret ballot, and there has been at least one occasion when a Senator has voted for a person from a different party to be President. Recently, the fact that no party has controlled the Senate has resulted in a sharing of power, with one major party having its nominee elected as President, and the other party providing the Chairman of Committees (the President's deputy).

The precarious voting position also makes it more likely that the President's ruling may be overturned when a dissent motion is proposed. However, such dissent motions occur less regularly than in the House. This is mainly because debate in the Senate tends to be less robust, and behaviour more orderly, than is the case in the House.

One major difference between the functions of the President and the Speaker is dictated by the Constitution. The Speaker only exercises a casting vote, so that he does not vote in ordinary divisions in the House of Representatives. If it is necessary for him to use his casting vote, he normally does so to allow the continuation of debate. However it has been very rare for the Speaker to need to use his casting vote in recent decades. The President, however, is expected to use his ordinary vote as a Senator in every division. He does not move from his chair, but his vote is counted and his name appears in every division list. But if the votes are equal he does not have a casting vote at all. A motion is defeated if the votes are equal.

The Chairman of Committees

In both the House of Representatives and the Senate a Chairman of Committees is elected who is in effect the deputy to the presiding officer. Their primary function is to take charge of the Chamber when the House or Senate moves 'into Committee'. This procedure does not involve splitting into groups. The House or the Senate can meet as a committee of the whole House. The aim is to make proceedings slightly less formal. This is indicated by the Chairman of Committees sitting below the Presiding Officer's chair, and between the clerks. In the House of Representatives he may be called by his name, rather than by his title. In both Chambers the move into committee is to allow detailed discussion on individual clauses in any proposed legislation, and the consideration of detailed amendments. When this consideration has been completed, the Speaker or President resumes his place and the Chairman of Committees formally reports to him what the Committee has decided. The House or Senate then has to adopt the report.

The Chairman of Committees does also sit in the place of the Speaker or President on occasions. He is the Acting Speaker or President if the Presiding Officer is overseas or unable to attend the Parliament, and takes over all the administrative responsibilities of the Speaker or President. When the President or Speaker leaves the Chair during the proceedings of the Parliament, he is normally the first of the various deputy or acting presiding officers to take his place.

Standing Orders

Over the years, both Houses have (separately) developed elaborate systems of rules to govern not only the way in which debate is conducted, but also every major element of procedure. The Standing

Orders set down the general order of business each day, and the way in which each is to be dealt with. They deal with what happens when a Member or Senator alleges that there has been a breach of parliamentary privilege, or what happens when an election result is disputed. They cover the procedure of parliamentary committees, the election of officers, and the recording of proceedings. In each House there are more than four hundred such Standing Orders but few of their members try to master them all. That is left to the officials and the officers of the Chambers, to advise the members or the Presiding Officers when necessary.

The Standing Orders of the House of Representatives were originally modelled on those of the House of Commons, and when an issue arises which is not covered by the Standing Orders, or by precedent, the House normally follows the rules of the House of Commons if they seem appropriate. The Senate's Standing Orders were based on those of the South Australian House of Assembly at the time of federation, because they were familiar to the first President of the Senate and could be administered by him without difficulty or delay. However, many changes have been made in both systems so that each is quite unique. It takes a little time for any parliamentarian changing from one House to the other (as sometimes happens) to become accustomed to the differences.

The Standing Orders lay down the general conduct of proceedings in a way which is not really neutral between the Government and the Opposition. All governments, of whatever political flavour, have seen advantage in adopting rules which are biased in such a way as to make life easier for the Government. For example, when a Minister proposes a motion, or introduces a Bill, he does not need to have someone else 'second' his motion; it is assumed that he has the necessary support. But an Opposition motion of any kind needs to be seconded before it can be considered. Another Standing Order prevents any debate whatsoever on a series of resolutions which are normally only moved by the Government—motions to adjourn a debate, or to gag a debate or to gag a member, or to suspend a member. Other Standing Orders give precedence most of the time to Government Business, and it is the Government which normally determines the order in which its business is considered. In the Senate, however, the Opposition's strength allows it to alter both the time available for Government Business and the order in which it is considered, if it presses the issue to a vote.

The rules which bring most complaint (but which have remained largely unaltered over the years) are those governing Question Time. In the House, there are fourteen separate restrictions on the content of a question. But the only limit to the answer is that it 'shall be relevant to the question', a requirement which Speakers inevitably interpret quite freely.

Precedent

Not every situation which arises in the Parliament is covered by the various Standing Orders. In those circumstances the Presiding Officers, advised by the Clerks, then have to take account of what has happened when similar situations have arisen in the past, and to follow the precedent which was then established in the form of a ruling by the then presiding officer. The Clerks keep detailed lists of the rulings which are made, and use these for guidance—unless of course a ruling is in turn overruled by a vote of dissent by the House, in which case it is the decision of the House which becomes the precedent which is to be followed the next time the incident occurs. It is by means of precedent, for example, that there has been built up a list of 'offensive' words which MPs and Senators are not permitted to use in the House—words like 'liar' or 'dishonest' when said of another Member or Senator, for example. The use of a 'disorderly' expression is usually met with a demand for a withdrawal, and if this is not given, the offending Member can find himself suspended from the Chamber. However, Members and Senators appear to find little difficulty in coming up with new expressions which manage to reflect on their opponents, and the presiding officers are always likely to be called on to rule about the acceptability of a particular insult which has been used.

Precedent, however, can always be overturned. An important example of this occurred in the Senate in the late 1960s when the then Liberal–Country Party Government lost its absolute majority in the Senate. One precedent, not incorporated in the Standing Orders, was that Question Time in the Senate should last for 45 minutes, and be ended whenever the Leader of the Government asked that further questions be placed on the Notice Paper. One day, after a particularly intensive set of questions directed against one of his Ministers, he 'moved' that further questions be placed on the Notice Paper. The Opposition insisted on a vote, and the motion was defeated. Question Time continued. It took some time for the Government to re-establish that Question Time should be limited to about 60 minutes in the Senate, and that it could be terminated by the Leader of the House saying that further questions should be placed on notice, it being accepted then that Ministers did have the right to decline to answer questions.

In recognition that the written rules do not provide a complete guide to the workings of the Parliament, a former Clerk of the

Senate compiled a book, *Australian Senate Practice*, which was published with the Senate's authority in 1953. It deals with virtually every issue likely to arise in the Senate, though it went through several editions (the fifth being published in 1976) to keep up with changes and developments in Senate practice. The House of Representatives published an even more massive compilation of practice and procedure for its Chamber in 1981. Together they cover most of the formal and informal rules by which the Parliament operates. But they cannot hope to cover how politicians use those rules.

CHAPTER 6

Symbols and Language (Baubles and Brawls)

The Chambers of the Commonwealth Parliament are largely modelled on those of the Palace of Westminster; but sometimes the language and behaviour and conduct of the Members is more suggestive of the Colosseum, or the 'outer' at a football game. Perhaps it is the contrast between the ornate and formal trappings, and the occasional 'bad' behaviour which so shocks some people. Newspapers which revel in reporting 'uproar' in the Parliament, then decry the standards of the Parliament, and invariably quote some visiting schoolchildren as saying that they wouldn't be allowed to behave that way in school.

Parliamentary history is highlighted by those occasions when the Parliament was a very rough place indeed. The British Parliament, so often held up as a model for all others to follow, has a bloody history. The House of Commons had to fight to assert its rights against the monarch. It precipitated and participated in a revolution. By comparison, the Australian Parliament's history has been boringly uneventful. But it is at times noisy, and the atmosphere does become highly charged. This is not surprising. The politicians who inhabit the Parliament are playing for very high stakes. Their decisions are likely to affect everyone in the nation. They are highly conscious of the likely impact of the laws they pass and the policies which the Government determines. They differ strongly about what many of those policies should be, and about which political party should wield the powers of Government. They believe that politics does matter, that it does make a great difference if one party rather than the other is in Government. They don't approach politics the way the true amateur sportsman is supposed to approach his game—for the sake of the game itself. They are not there because the game itself is fun, or satisfying. They are there to win. They want to be in

Government not Opposition. They want their own policies, not someone else's, to be implemented. They want to make decisions themselves, not have someone else making them. Tensions and emotions and political feeling often run very high. If the language the politicians use is occasionally very boisterous, at least the politicians do not come to blows, or fight one another in the aisles, as has occurred in some other British parliaments, and may still occur in some other countries.

The people who get elected to Parliament are there because they have strong feelings about politics or political issues, far stronger than the feelings of the man or woman in the street, or of the people who come to watch the politicians in the Parliament. Politicians often sacrifice careers to get into Parliament and to work for their political goals, and many of them actually earn less as parliamentarians than they would had they remained outside Parliament. They risk being defeated at every election—even those in 'safe' seats can have their party endorsements withdrawn, forcing them into an early retirement from the Parliament. Worse still, they can face oblivion within the Parliament, on the Opposition benches, frustrated at their inability to influence the way the country is run, and helpless to stop their opponents from over-turning laws and policies which their own side introduced when it was in Government. It is not surprising that there are occasional angry outbursts of frustration and rage.

The trappings

The British Parliament at Westminster set the tone and the style of furnishing all of the Australian parliaments, but particularly the Parliament in Canberra. The House of Representatives, like the House of Commons, is furnished with green upholstery and green carpets. The Senate, like the House of Lords, is decked out in red.

In the House of Representatives, the Speaker's Chair is an elaborately carved replica of the original House of Commons' Speaker's Chair. It has a 'foliated' canopy, and intricate carvings and mouldings. Above the Chair are the Royal Arms, carved in oak taken from the roof of Westminster Hall. The arm-rests are carved from oak from Nelson's flagship, HMS *Victory*. On the central table near the clerks' chairs are two large despatch boxes, which have elaborate silver and enamel decorations. These were a gift from King George V, for the opening of the Parliament in 1927. The despatch boxes were exact copies of those in the House of Commons, which were later to be destroyed when the House of

The Speaker's Chair, a sand-glass, despatch box and the mace

Commons was bombed in 1941. The boxes have no practical use other than to provide a resting place for the notes of Ministers or shadow Ministers (who speak from the despatch box). In more dramatic moments, they are sometimes thumped by those same speakers.

Another gift from the British Parliament is the mace, the symbol of the authority of the Speaker and of the House, and originally a symbol of Royal authority. Once again, the gift followed the design of the mace used in the House of Commons. Normally the mace is placed on a stand on the main table in the centre of the House when it is in session, but below the table when the House is in Committee. In the past, however, there have been some Speakers who would not allow it to be displayed at all. One Speaker referred to it as a 'relic of barbarism' and said it was associated with methods and manners that should have no place in public life.

Traditional styles extend beyond the furnishings. While the mace is a symbol of authority, so to is the person who used to wield it in battle, the Serjeant-at-Arms. The Royal Serjeant-at-Arms was an important person in the evolution of the power of the House of Commons. In the 14th and early 15th centuries, the Royal Serjeants-at-Arms were extremely powerful, having powers of arrest without warrant and an ability to influence the administration of the Courts. They drew their authority from the King, and the mace, stamped with the royal arms, was the symbol of their power. In the early 15th century the Commons persuaded the King to assign one of the Serjeants-at-Arms to the House of Commons, to protect its authority and its privileges. A century later the Commons was able to use its Serjeant and his authority, to free one of its members who had been imprisoned by the sheriffs of the City of London.

The Serjeant-at-Arms has no independent source of power in Australia, though he does exercise the authority of the House to maintain order among the public who enter the Parliament, and to conduct members who have been suspended from the House. To indicate the ancient origins of his office, the Serjeant-at-Arms on ceremonial occasions wears traditional Court dress, knee breeches, buckled shoes, lace jabot and cuffs, gloves and a sword, and carries a cocked hat.

A similar display is affected by the equivalent officer in the Senate, Black Rod, whose office was established in the House of Lords by Henry VIII. In Britain the job is still filled by a personal appointee of the sovereign, but in Australia Black Rod is a member of the Department of the Senate staff.

Usher of the Black Rod

Ceremonial dress is also available to the Speaker and the President. They are entitled to wear a black Queen's Counsel's silk gown, full bottomed judge's wig and lace cuffs and jabot. These are still worn by Liberal Party incumbents of those offices, but not by Labor men.

The Clerks in both Houses also wear formal clothes, based on the dress of barristers, with bob-wig and gown, but with white evening bow tie and stiff collar and bands.

In one very important sense there has been a break with the traditions of the Palace of Westminster. This concerns the shape and the size of the Chambers. In Westminster, the House of Commons is in a long, narrow hall, with seating arranged in tiered banks on either side. There are no permament places for members, and indeed there are not sufficient places for all the MPs. This tradition was maintained after the House was destroyed during the second world war. Prime Minister Churchill maintained that the smaller Chamber was conducive to proper debate. The House of Representatives and the Senate, however, were designed to be occupied by members of Parliament who were full-time parliamentarians and, in any event, the Chambers in the Canberra Parliament House had to accommodate far fewer Members and Senators than did those in Westminster. The smaller size of the Chambers makes it practicable for Members to be counted in their places when a vote is taken, instead of having to move out of the Chamber and to file through division lobbies.

Further compromises with tradition have come with the advent of technology. Telephones (in the colour appropriate to the Chamber concerned) now stand among the ancient despatch boxes. Microphones are set on the centre table and around the Chambers, to broadcast proceedings. Although divisions are timed by means of sand-glasses, clocks time the speeches of Members and Senators, and warn them just how much of their speaking time remains. In the House of Representatives television cameras record the proceedings, though their images are available only on monitors in the offices of the whips and the Leader of the House and his opposite number. A similar television facility is provided in the Senate for the Leader of Government Business, his opposite number and the whips.

Behaviour

For the most part, politicians play out the dignified roles in which the furnishings and fittings have set them. They obey the written and unwritten rules. They make their speeches to Mr Speaker, or Mr President, as if trying to persuade him, rather than their fellow parliamentarians or the public at large. They refer, in the House, to other Members according to the electorates they represent: 'The Honourable Member for Sydney'. All other Members and Senators are 'Honourable' (at least within the precincts of the House or Senate) and a few are even 'Right Honourable' (those who are members of Her Majesty's Privy Council, an honour not given under Labor Governments). The Speaker is always called Mr Speaker, the President always Mr President, though both, while they hold office, are entitled to the title, the Honourable.

When Members or Senators enter or leave their Chamber, they bow to the Presiding Officer, as a mark of respect. They are not permitted to stand around in the Chamber while a debate is in progress, or to speak except from their own place in the Chamber (except that a Minister or shadow Minister may speak from the centre table, by a despatch box. Good speeches may not be applauded, but in the best British tradition, approval may be indicated by saying 'hear hear'. (The public, in the galleries, is not allowed to express any noise of any kind, or demonstrate in any way.) There is no standard way of indicating disapproval, but again the British tradition of calling 'shame' is sometimes followed, or 'resign' if the disapproval is being directed at a Government Minister. Less formal calls across the Chamber (more akin to the barracking which might be heard at a football match) are common, but rarely get a mention in *Hansard*.

During Question Time, Members seeks to attract the Speaker's attention so that they can get his call to ask a question. They do this by standing in their places, hoping to catch his eye. Some do so rather noisily, trying to attract his ear as well, while others try to prompt him by calling out 'Mr Speaker'. In fact, the Speaker has a list on which he marks off the names of Members as they ask questions during a parliamentary sitting, to try to help him distribute questions as evenly as possible among those who wish to ask them. There are, however, some exceptions. He distributes questions alternately between the Opposition and Government backbenchers, and he distributes them within the Liberal-National coalition in the ratio of two questions for Liberals to one question for Nationals (again, with the intention of trying to balance out the numbers).

In ordinary debates, catching the Speaker's eye is much less of a problem. The Speaker is given by the whips a list of those who are to speak in the debate, in the order in which they are to speak.

Politeness and orderly behaviour predominate. Most of the time Members and Senators act in accordance with the best traditions of the Parliament, and the etiquette which is spelt out for them in the Senate and House of Representatives Practice books. But disruption, disorder and abusive language occur in spasms, and provide the real test of a Speaker's ability. Such bouts might occur several times a week, and last anything from a few minutes to an hour.

A fall from elegant standards of behaviour may be touched off by a personal reflection on a Member, or a misrepresentation of a party's policy, or a restriction of the Opposition's ability to debate a particular issue. Or it may be the result of a deliberate Opposition tactic, aimed at drawing attention to something it has been unable to dramatise in any other way. Almost invariably it will be the Opposition which causes the rumpus, even though it may have been provoked by something that a Minister has said, or the Government has done.

The disorder may take many forms. A Member may use 'unparliamentary' language and not immediately withdraw it, he may continue to interject when he has been warned to stop, or try to speak and call out when he does not have the call. The unparliamentary language may go beyond the almost acceptable words like 'liar' and make serious imputations, such as that some member of the other side is a 'crook' or has broken the law or cheated the income tax. The fracas usually develops with the Speaker demanding 'Order!' and getting no response; with the side which thinks it has been improperly abused demanding a withdrawal or a retraction of the offending remarks; and with the person responsible for the outcry refusing to withdraw and trying to proceed with his remarks, or even to justify them. A great many people will be calling out at the same time. Typically, Members from both sides will be trying to attract the Speaker's attention so as to take a 'point of order' (that is, they will be trying to persuade the Speaker that something that the other side has done is contrary to some provision in the official Standing Orders). Eventually, the Speaker will have to make rulings on these various points of order, and decide whether particular remarks were offensive or unparliamentary and have to be withdrawn. Once a ruling is made, the Opposition can challenge it by moving dissent from the Speaker's ruling. Such a motion allows the Opposition leadership to explain what it is they are complaining about, though the Speaker on occasions may provoke even further uproar by trying to limit the ground which can be covered in those speeches. The Government would normally gag the debate on the dissent motion, and there would be a vote on that gag, and then a vote on the motion, and all these proceedings would have used up the whole of the time set aside for Question Time—at which point almost everyone leaves the Chamber and the House resumes its normal routine.

Another possible outcome of a confrontation in the House is a refusal by the offending Member to withdraw remarks which have been ruled unparliamentary, or a refusal to obey some other ruling by the Speaker, or warnings by him to stop interjecting. After several warnings (usually) the Speaker will then 'name' the particular offender (simply by saying, 'I name the Honourable Member for xyz'). At that point the Leader of the House then moves 'That the Honourable Member for xyz be suspended from the services of the House' and a vote is immediately taken. The Member is escorted from the Chamber by the Serjeant-at-Arms, and cannot return for 24 hours, during which time he is not supposed to use any of the facilities of the Parliament. If he is suspended twice in the same sittings, the suspension is for a week, rather than a day. A suspension tends to be good for a headline in the Member's local paper.

Some Members develop a reputation for their willingness to 'drop buckets' on Members on the other side, either through asking questions designed to highlight personal or political peccadilloes, or through their willingness to use speeches on the adjournment or at other times to indulge in personal attacks. Such speeches may not even infringe the rules. But they generally result in the raising of tensions in the House, and a spate of rowdy scenes. However, not very many MPs are very good in verbal rough-house situations. Occasionally confrontations develop when otherwise mild-mannered MPs are quite genuinely grievously offended by something said or done by someone on the other side about some issue in which he has some deep personal involvement (for example, in relation to religious or racial discrimination, or migration).

Not all disruptions to the smooth flow of parliamentary business are against the rules. The Standing Orders have many provisions which an Opposition can exploit to waste time and disturb the Government's arrangements for the Parliament. Many of the arrangements in the House or the Senate depend on obtaining 'leave' to do something—for someone to speak out of order, or for a motion to be put which has not been properly notified, or for progress to the next stage of a Bill to be made immediately. 'Leave' means the approval of all the Members, and it needs only one to call out 'no' and that leave is refused. The Government then has to move for the suspension of part of the Standing Orders to allow it to proceed as it wishes, and if a vote is insisted on, more time is taken. Requiring a vote is one of the most effective time-wasting devices open to the Opposition, and it is also highly disruptive for Ministers and backbenchers who have to leave meetings or appointments and hurry into the Chamber.

The same disruption occurs when a Member calls for a quorum. A quorum is one-third of the total membership of the House. Any Member can at any time 'draw the Speaker's attention to the state of the House'. The Speaker (assisted by his clerks) then counts the number of Members present in the Chamber. If there are fewer than the necessary one-third, the Speaker orders that the bells be rung (these being the same bells as are used to call Members into a Division). The word is quickly shouted down the Opposition corridors that there is a quorum, not a division, and Opposition members heed the call by remaining outside the Chamber. This means that the task of providing the numbers falls entirely on the Government. Cabinet meetings and committees break all over Parliament House as Ministers and backbenchers alike hurry to the Chamber. As soon as the quorum is filled, the Speaker calls on the ordinary business to proceed, and the House quickly empties again—until the next quorum call. If the quorum is not met within the two minutes allowed, the House is said to have been 'counted out', and has to be adjourned by the Speaker—to the Government's very great embarrassment. It is almost equally embarrassing for a person who calls a quorum to discover that there was actually a quorum present in the House when he drew the Speaker's attention to the state of the House. Such a false alarm normally earns a suspension for 24 hours. Quorum calls are sometimes the result of a deliberate Opposition policy to annoy the Government, but they can also be brought on by individual Opposition backbenchers who want to disrupt the speech of a particular Government MP. The quorum call is a device which has no real counterpart in the British Parliament, where the quorum is only forty MPs in a House of about 650 Members. If the House of Representatives had the same proportionate requirement, a quorum would be satisfied with about nine MPs, instead of almost fifty.

Much of the misbehaviour may seem petty or even childish. The institution, however, constrains and controls the political conflict within civilised bounds. One former Deputy Prime Minister said that the idea of political conflict was that 'if you see a head, kick it'. Parliament ensures that type of reaction does not occur in a direct physical way, but only metaphorically. The misbehaviour which is seen or heard in Parliament is mostly quite controlled and in accordance with the standards of behaviour associated with real parliaments where the participants are playing real politics.

CHAPTER 7

Committees of the Parliament

Some of the Parliament's most valuable work is done outside the formal chambers of the House of Representatives and the Senate. The work is performed by scores of committees, some established by the Parliament as a whole, some by the Senate and the House separately. A few of the committees are very small, with only four or five members. The largest has twenty-one members. Four of the Committees are regarded as so important that they were established under separate Acts of Parliament, but most are created by agreement between the two Houses, or under the Standing Orders of the Houses. All the committees contain representatives from Government and Opposition parties, and the Senate committees usually contain a representative of one of the smaller parties also. Most of the committees manage to avoid taking partisan political positions on the subjects they are investigating and present reports to the Parliament which have been unanimously agreed upon, across party lines.

The work the committees do is extraordinarily varied. Some examine the annual Budget in detail, others look at expenditures, and another looks at the general financial administration of all Government Departments. Some examine the effectiveness of Government policies, others look at specific proposals for Government action. Committees examine such subjects as foreign affairs and defence, the environment and Aboriginal welfare. One examines the nature of all proposed legislation to see that it does not interfere with personal rights and liberties. Another looks at Government building proposals, to ensure that they are necessary and that they are to be carried out as efficiently as possible.

Some committees are appointed to carry out a special task—an investigation into a particular policy or a particular problem—and then cease to exist when they have finished their reports. A few have been created on a permanent basis, their powers and responsibilities defined in laws which envisage that they will always have a function to perform. But most are appointed and then re-appointed at the beginning of each new Parliament, and from time to time specific tasks are added to their general responsibilities in well-defined areas. Most of the committees meet in public to take evidence, and in private to consider what recommendations or decisions they should make.

Ministers rarely participate in the work of the committees except as witnesses, answering queries about their budget proposals or about the administration of their Departments. To some extent, committee work is seen as a consolation prize for backbenchers who have not been chosen or elected as Ministers. Committee work gives them the chance to make a real contribution to policy development and government administration, and can provide conscientious members with a great measure of satisfaction in performing a responsible job. Committee work is often seen as a proper extension of the Parliament's role in scrutinising the work of the executive. For some committees, the work is part of the Parliament's legislative process.

Committees certainly keep backbenchers busy. On average, Senators sit on about three Senate or joint committees; MPs sit on an average of one committee.

Much of the committee work is of comparatively recent origin. Committees became fashionable towards the end of the 1960s, mainly through the efforts of Senators (primarily the Labor leaders and Liberal backbenchers) and Senate staff. In 1970 two sets of Senate standing committees were created on a trial basis— one group to examine the various Departmental estimates which were presented to the Parliament along with the Budget and Supply Bills, and another group which were to look at policy and administrative problems associated with the whole range of Governmental activity. What made the creation of the committees possible was the loss by the then Liberal–Country Party Government of its majority in the Senate, and the recognition by the Labor Party and the minor parties that there were considerable political benefits to be obtained from committee investigation into politically sensitive areas. The committees passed the tests laid down for them and have now become a permanent feature of Senate committee work.

At the same time a large number of select committees were established to examine particular problems, and one of those committees, the Senate Committee on Security and Exchange (known as the Rae Committee after Senator Peter Rae, who chaired it for most of its existence) achieved such public notice that parliamentary committee work came into both public and parliamentary vogue. The Rae committee was formed in the wake of a stock market crash of some mining companies. All the principal characters in the affair were interviewed by the committee both in private and in public, the public hearings attracting an enormous amount of media and public attention. The committee did not restrict itself to the scandal which had been the cause of its establishment, but went on to investigate in great detail the way in which the securities industry was organised and regulated. The main effect of its work was to create the environment for a combined national and state regulatory régime, which eventually emerged in the form of the National Companies and Securities Commission.

The most permanent committees are those which are established under laws passed by the whole Parliament. These committees continue from Parliament to Parliament without the need to be re-created, though after every election each of the Houses has to renominate the parliamentarians who sit on the committees.

The Joint Committee on Public Accounts (known as the PAC) has sixteen members and has an extremely wide brief to investigate Commonwealth Government finances. It can examine all the accounts of receipts and expenditure by Commonwealth Government Departments and authorities and reports by the Auditor-General. The committee is not intended to look at the policies which the Government implements, but with the administrative and financial administration. For example, the committee is not concerned to examine whether the Government was right in choosing to buy a particular type of aircraft for the RAAF, but it is concerned to see that it does not pay too much, or waste money on equipment which is unnecessary, or buys the wrong equipment to service it. The Committee spends a great deal of time following up investigations by the Auditor-General which have revealed flaws in Departmental administration or financial irregularities. The committee's reports are followed up by the Department of Finance, which has to prepare minutes giving instructions to Departments on any upgrading of their financial or administrative procedures. The Committee then examines the Department of Finance minutes to see whether they conform with the Committee's recommendations.

The Committee also conducts investigations using sub-committees of its own members into areas of general or specific administration. In 1985 it had three sub-committees: one was investigating medical fraud and overservicing, another the management of major defence equipment acquisitions, and a third, automatic data processing.

The oldest of the Joint Statutory committees is the Public Works Committee, which was created by the Parliament in 1913. Its task is to examine and report on all major proposed construction works to be undertaken by the Commonwealth. From June 1985 the Committee was required to examine all proposed works costing $6 million or more—though some important statutory authorities do not come under its supervision, authorities such as the National Capital Development Commission (responsible for most construction of Commonwealth works in Canberra), TAA, Qantas, and the Australian National Railways. Even without these authorities to examine, the Committee is kept very busy, averaging about fifteen reports a year. The committee travels extensively throughout Australia and its territories (in 1981 it spent three days in the Antarctic examining a proposal to improve facilities at the Australian Antarctic base) and holds most of its hearings in public. It provides a second opinion for the Government, utilising the views of expert outsiders to critically review construction projects. Nor is it limited strictly to engineering or architectural aspects of a construction project. An airport works proposal will also normally involve considerations of access and airport noise and town planning.

The third of the Joint Statutory committees is the Committee on the broadcasting of Parliament. Its duties have mainly been to decide on which days the various Houses would be broadcast by the ABC, and to generally supervise those broadcasts. However, the Committee has begun inquiring into possible extensions of the way in which the Parliament is broadcast, both on radio and television. A report in 1985 resulted in the introduction of an experiment to allow radio and television to use voice recording extracts in news and current affairs programs. The committee is also investigating the possible televising of Parliament on a regular basis.

The latest of the statutory committees was established in 1984, as part of the legislation creating the National Crime Authority. The new committee is intended to keep a watch on the committee's work and to ensure that it is not unduly fettered.

The two Houses of the Parliament have several other joint committees which although not enshrined in legislation have proved to be long-lasting. One is a committee on the Australian

Capital Territory, which has as a continuing function the examination of changes in the formal plan of Canberra—changes which generally involve the creation of new suburbs or the alterations of streets. More controversial is the joint Foreign Affairs and Defence Committee, which during the 1960s was boycotted by the Labor Party. The committee has conducted investigations into Australian relations with southeast Asia and in 1985 had three inquiries under way, one of them into disarmament and arms control.

Another joint committee is looking after the Parliament's general interests in the new Parliament House.

The Parliament also forms joint select committees to examine specific problems. In 1985 there were two such committees, one into electoral reform, the other into video material.

The greatest array of Parliamentary committees is in the Senate, where in mid-1985 there were four select committees, nine standing committees, eight legislative and general purpose standing committees and six estimates committees. Some of the standing committees deal only with what are essentially domestic management problems—the House committee, the library committee, publications, standing orders, and appropriations and staffing. One is the privileges committee, which considers allegations of breaches of parliamentary privilege and recommends any penalties to the full Senate when it finds there have been breaches (see Chapter 10 on the powers of the Parliament to punish people for contempt).

One of the oldest and most important of the standing committees is the Regulations and Ordinances Committee. This was established in 1932 to try to supervise the enormous number of regulations and by-laws made by the executive government under powers given to it by the Parliament. These regulations are intended to flesh out the details of the laws passed by Parliament. But the Senate was concerned to ensure that the regulations did not infringe on civil liberties, or by-pass parliamentary control. The material the committee examines (with the assistance of professional legal advisers) is of a greater volume than all the Acts passed by Parliament in a year. The committee's examination is based on four principles:

- to ensure that the delegated legislation is in accordance with the law which authorises it;
- to ensure that it does not trespass unduly on personal rights and liberties;
- to ensure that it does not unduly make the rights and liberties of

citizens dependent on administrative decisions which are not subject to review on their merits by a judicial or other independent tribunal;
- to ensure that it does not contain matter more appropriate to be included in an Act of Parliament.

The Committee's recommendations carry great weight because the Senate has the power to set aside any of the mass of regulations. Normally, when it finds some aspect of a regulation of which it disapproves, it discusses it with the appropriate Minister or his Department, and tries to have the regulation changed. But occasionally the Senate has to use its full power to disallow the regulation.

The Committee's work rarely makes headlines, but it is a model for other Parliaments, both in Australia and overseas, which have become concerned about the amount of law-making which takes place away from the direct control of the Parliament.

It was not until the 1980s that the Senate was able to establish a committee to review ordinary legislation in the light of the same kind of principles which guides the Regulations and Ordinances Committee's review of subordinate laws. Titled the Scrutiny of Bills committee, its terms included reviewing all laws introduced into the Parliament to see whether they would:
- trespass unduly on personal rights and liberties;
- make rights and liberties unduly dependent on insufficiently defined or non-reviewable administrative decisions;
- inappropriately delegate legislative power or make it insufficiently subject to parliamentary scrutiny.

The committee reports to the Senate on all Bills which contain clauses which violate the principles, providing a new focus for debate in the Senate. The fact that the committee makes such an examination has made Government Departments far more careful about the provisions they include in legislation, and the fact that the Senate is prepared to amend Bills to enforce the principles has made Ministers much more likely to change their proposals before the Senate does the changing for them.

The eight Legislative and General Purpose committees are concerned with policy issues which range across the whole Government administration. The committees examine all the annual reports of Government Departments and authorities, and in addition any specific tasks given to them by the Senate. The committee on finance and Government administration is particularly concerned with the operation, administration and accountability of statutory authorities—ranging from the organisations

involved in transport (TAA, Qantas and Australian National Railways) through to the Commonwealth Superannuation Fund, and the ABC. The other Legislative and General Purpose committees are:
- constitutional and legal affairs;
- education and the arts;
- foreign affairs and defence;
- industry and trade;
- national resources;
- science, technology and the environment; and
- social welfare.

The range of committees in the House of Representatives is not nearly as great as that in the Senate. Although there was some concern in the House when the Senate went through its committee boom in the early 1970s, and official suggestions were made that the House should have a similar range of committees, this did not obtain the support of either Liberal or Labor Governments, which both preferred a smaller increase in the number of House committees. The House experimented with the creation of legislation committees, which were intended to take over the detailed committee stage consideration of Bills. But these were not persevered with. The most significant of the committees which has survived is the Committee on Expenditure, which is particularly concerned with investigating the reports by the Auditor-General on the efficiency of Government Departments and instrumentalities. Other committees established by the House are on Aboriginal affairs; environment and conservation; transport safety; Aboriginal education; and aircraft noise. There is also a range of 'House' committees paralleling those in the Senate on domestic matters: the House committee. the library committee, privileges committee, and a committee on Members' interests.

One of the limitations on committee work is the availability of members or senators to work on them. The average Senate committee, for example, met in 1984 on about fifty days, and for more than three hours at each such meeting. And each Senator sat on at least three committees. The Committees also need to be serviced by staff provided mainly by the Senate and House of Representatives committee staff. The input by the staff depends on the subject-matter and the interests and knowledge of the individual committee members. Many of the committees also need to employ consultants and legal counsel to provide the expertise necessary if the reports of the committees are to be of a high quality.

Those who serve on the committees have been anxious to

ensure that their work has not been ignored by successive Governments. The Senate has set aside at least an hour each week for the debating of Senate reports—one way of ensuring that the Senate itself can apply pressure through publicity. Governments have responded by promising not to pigeon-hole the reports prepared by the various committees. All Governments have undertaken to respond within six months to the report of a committee—though response does not necessarily involve acceptance of all of the recommendations of a report.

The reason for the blossoming of the committee system owed a lot to political opportunism, and to the frustration of otherwise underworked backbenchers. But the committees were also intended to serve very real parliamentary purposes. The Clerk of the Senate in 1970 explained that the committee system needed to be expanded to allow the Senate to cope with:

1. increasing Governmental responsibilities and activities;
2. the impact of the tremendous progress in science and technology;
3. the complexity of legislation which cannot always be satisfactorily considered within narrow parliamentary timetables;
4. the inadequacy of opportunities and means on the floor of the House to discharge fully Parliament's important duty to probe and check the administration;
5. the inadequacy of present-day means for the ventilation of citizens' grievances against administrative decisions or acts;
6. growing executive expertise and secrecy;
7. the need, in an increasingly expert world, for parliamentarians to be able to call on scholarly research and advice equal in competence to that relied upon by the administration.

CHAPTER 8

Parties and Party Committees

The way the Australian Parliament works is largely determined by the nature of the political parties which operate in it, and in particular by their rigidity and tight discipline. The focus is always on politics—the politics of trying to win Government or to hold on to Government. Party unity is seen as an important means towards that end, and often as an end in itself.

Since 1901 more than 99 per cent of all the members of the Commonwealth Parliament have been members of political parties, and most of them have been members of the three major political parties. The Australian parliamentary system is based on the operation of those political parties. It is almost always possible to predict with absolute accuracy the result of any vote in the Parliament, because Australian parliamentarians almost always vote with their party. That takes a lot of the drama out of parliamentary proceedings. The 'winner' on any issue is almost never in doubt (though the fact, that these days, the Government party is unlikely to have a majority in the Senate, means that the fate of particular pieces of legislation can be very much in doubt). The combination of almost universal membership by MPs of political parties, and the highly disciplined nature of those parties, means that often it looks as though the MPs are simply going through the motions of debate, or voting. The result is effectively pre-ordained by the size of the various parties in the Parliament, and what is said and done by MPs in the Parliament does not seem to matter very much—at least in so far as the outcome of a particular parliamentary proceeding is concerned.

This is very different from the situation in the British Parliament where MPs are quite likely to vote against their party (or abstain from voting) at some time in the Parliament, though not as regularly as U.S. Congressmen and Senators are expected to do so.

Every British Government since World War II has had to withdraw important legislation from the Parliament in the face of hostility from its own side to that legislation. Governments with a majority in the House of Commons have sometimes seen several pieces of legislation a year defeated as a result of the defection of some of their own supporters. Such defections simply do not occur in the House of Representatives. The tight Australian discipline and voting pattern means that it is not at all difficult for a Government to survive in the House of Representatives with a floor majority of only one Member, without much chance of losing any votes during a three-year term. That does not affect the amount of effort which the political leaders—Prime Minister, Ministers, Opposition Leader and shadow Ministers—put into their performances in the Parliament. Their efforts are devoted both to trying to persuade the public of the correctness of their own policies and the faults of their opponents, and to trying to impress their supporters, inside and outside the Parliament, of their strengths as political leaders.

But the largely predetermined nature of what happens in the Parliament means that backbenchers who want to make an impact on policy creation and development, and on the shape of legislation, are likely to devote most of their efforts elsewhere—outside the parliamentary chambers. For many parliamentarians, particularly Senators, parliamentary committees (referred to in the previous chapter) provide them with their best opportunities. For others, there are even more fruitful prospects given to them through the way their own political party operates within the Parliament. Much of the policy investigation and the amendment of proposed laws which would have happened in the Parliament itself in the days before the present strong party system developed, now occurs within the various parliamentary parties—in the party rooms and party committee meetings.

It is only very recently that the role of political parties in the parliamentary system came to be properly recognised in a formal, legal way. Previously, the role of the parties had been an unwritten part of the system, one of the 'conventions' which helped the system to work. In 1983, however, the Parliament passed changes to the Electoral Act which provide for such things as the putting of names of political parties on ballot papers, and the payment of public funds to the parties for election expenses (these are dealt with in the section dealing with elections in Chapter 13).

Despite the previous absence of full legislative recognition of the role of the political parties in the parliamentary system, the whole procedure of the Parliament has long been based on the functioning of major political parties. Where people sit in the Parliament depends on which party they belong to, and whether that party has enough members to make up a majority of the membership of the House of Representatives, and so be the Government. It is the parties which organise who is to take part in the various debates in Parliament. It is the parties' choice of their leader which gives the voters the two candidates for Prime Minister—the Liberal leader or the Labor leader.

Another recognition of the significance of the role of political parties in the Parliament is that party leaders are paid additional allowances, and so are party whips—the people who are responsible for ensuring that all a party's members attend Parliament at the right time (or if they are absent, that they are 'paired' with a party member from a different party so that the voting balance between the two sides won't be altered) and who are responsible for drawing up speaking lists and, within the chambers, for counting those taking part in divisions.

Even more significantly, Parliament's weekly timetable is arranged is such a way that a morning is specially put aside for the parties to have their separate meetings. These meetings are in a sense quite the most important non-parliamentary activities which occur in Parliament and are intended to affect what happens in the Parliament.

Party decision-making

The Labor Party has adopted more stringent rules concerning the powers of its party meetings and the party's control over the activities of its members in the Parliament than have the other parties. But, in practice, all the parties tend to behave in a similar way

The Labor Party organisation makes formal provision for what it calls 'The Federal Parliamentary Labor Party' (or FPLP) and what everyone calls the Caucus.[5] The only body in the Labor Party which can give directions to the FPLP is the party's National Conference or National Executive, but the attitude usually taken

[5] Strictly speaking, the word caucus means a meeting of the parliamentary members of any political party, to determine the party's tactics. But the word has different meanings in different places. It is used in New Zealand in its general sense to refer to parliamentary meetings of both major political parties. In Britain it is used in a somewhat derogatory way, to refer to any local party group which exercises control over its parliamentary candidate. In Australia it is generally used to refer only to the parliamentary Labor Party.

by those bodies is that they should lay down general policies, and the FPLP should determine how and when they should be implemented. (On those occasions when the National Conference or Executive has taken a more dictatorial attitude to the parliamentary party, there has usually been a major row in the ALP.) But it is the rules of the Caucus itself which determine the power of the Caucus, coupled with the pledge given by Labor MPs and Senators seeking election, to 'vote as a majority of the Labor Party may decide in a Caucus meeting'. The Caucus rules also require its members to vote in Parliament in accordance with the decisions of Caucus—they also make it compulsory for each Labor MP and Senator to attend Parliament and vote for whatever Caucus has decided (unless a member is given leave by the Leader). This means it is as improper for a Labor MP to abstain from voting (or to walk out of the House to avoid voting) as it is for him to vote against his party.

The other side of this tight-discipline coin, is that every member of the Caucus has an equal say in what the party does in the Parliament. The backbencher's vote is the equal of that of the Prime Minister (though his voice will not necessarily be as persuasive!).

The most important task the Caucus faces after each election is to elect its leaders. After a successful election, this is unlikely to create much of a problem, at least so far as the Parliamentary Leader and his deputy is concerned. If successful at the polls, they have already become accepted in the public mind at least, as Prime Minister and Deputy Prime Minister. The next problem, though, is the selection of the parliamentary executive. When in Opposition, these, together with the Leader and his deputy, form the shadow Ministry. In Government they make up the Ministry and a number of them (the exact number is determined by the Caucus) form the Cabinet, while the remaining Ministers are in the outer Ministry. Although the Caucus chooses which of its members will be Ministers (or shadow Ministers) the jobs they are to do (their portfolios or shadow Ministry positions) are allocated by the party leader.

During the parliamentary year, the Caucus usually meets each week for about three hours. It begins by considering legislation which is to come before the Parliament, it hears a report from its leader, following which members may question any member of the Caucus executive (that is, any Minister if Labor is in Government, or shadow Minister if it is in Opposition), and then it considers any general business. This last would involve the discussion of any matters which members have notified they want the party to discuss or make decisions on, and could include policy matters or organisational issues. The meeting then considers any reports or recommendations from its officers or from committee chairmen.

What is significant is that in all these matters Caucus is making decisions which are binding on all its members—which means, when it is in Government, binding on the Prime Minister, his Cabinet and his Ministers, as well as the remainder of Caucus. There is no room for dissent once decisions have been made (though Cabinet may get a matter reconsidered by Caucus if, for example, after considering the Caucus decision, it can come up with a proposal for which it can get majority support in Caucus). Caucus decisions can affect a great deal of what the Government does though, strictly speaking, the only matters which are required to go to Caucus for decision are those which require some parliamentary action, usually in the form of legislation. But whatever Labor does in Parliament (aside from following its leaders in purely tactical motions relating to the conduct of Parliament itself) is conclusively decided and determined by the Caucus.

That approach is based on the party's history and experience. The Labor Party was created by trade unions to send delegates into Parliament to try to protect the general interests of the labor movement. The impetus for its creation was provided by Australia's first nationwide strikes, on the waterfront and in the pastoral industry, in 1890–91. Those who were elected to Parliament in the 1890s by the labor movement were expected to pledge their allegiance to labor principles—there were real fears that, once in Parliament, those elected would simply play parliamentary games, instead of trying to advance the labor cause. Labor's experiences over the following ninety or so years appeared to justify some of these fears. The Labor Party went through three major splits, and on two of those occasions, and once when there was not a general split, its leader shifted to the other side of politics to become (or remain as) Prime Minister. Labor's splits have sometimes been caused by the ambitions of individuals and sometimes by its desire to maintain its ideological purity, even at the expense of office.

The Liberal Party's origins and history are very different from those of the A.L.P. Until 1908 there were two major anti-Labor parties represented in the federal Parliament, the one favouring free trade, the other protectionism. They fought each other as strongly as they fought the Labor Party—indeed the Liberal Government of Alfred Deakin from 1905 to 1908 was kept in power by the votes of the Labor Party. When that Government was defeated, however, the anti-Labor parties went through a 'fusion' taking on the Liberal Party name. In 1917 the Liberals, who were in Opposition, supported Labor Prime Minister W. M. Hughes when he and a small group split from the Labor Party over the issue of conscription for overseas military service. In 1918 the Liberals and Hughes and his supporters formed a new party, the Nationalists, under Hughes's leadership until 1923, when a new party which was to go into coalition with the Nationalists, the Country Party, insisted on Hughes stepping down as Prime Minister and party leader. The next change of name of the party occurred in 1932, after Labor had won its first election since World War I, but had to deal with the crisis of the Depression. Several senior Ministers deserted the Labor Party to join with the Nationalists as the United Australia Party under the leadership of Lyons, the former Labor Deputy Prime Minister. The last reorganisation of the major anti-Labor party occurred in 1945, when it became the Liberal Party again, following the break up of the UAP after the defeat of the Menzies Government in 1941.

One of the central tenets of the new Liberal Party was that its parliamentarians should be independent of any 'outside' control. But freedom from outside control does not necessarily result in a lack of discipline among the members of the party inside the Parliament. It is uncommon for Liberals elected to Parliament to vote other than along party lines. A number of Liberal Senators were able to ignore the wishes of the party leadership and vote against occasional measures proposed by Liberal Governments in the 1960s, partly because they had strong backing from their home States. But, more recently, any suggestion that a Liberal MP would vote against his party has been met with the threat that the party leadership would do its best to ensure that he was deprived of his party endorsement, which would presumably cost him his seat in Parliament.

While the Labor Caucus as a whole is responsible for the stance take by Labor MPs and Senators in the Parliament, the Liberal Party meeting leaves most decision making to its Leader. In theory, the one and only conclusive decision which the Liberal Party meeting takes is its election of a Leader. The party then delegates to him the choice of Ministers or shadow Ministers (apart from the Deputy Leader, who is also elected by the party). The regular weekly party meeting (held in conjunction with the National Party) reviews the parliamentary program and offers backbenchers a chance to question the party's leaders and Ministers or shadow Ministers. The party meeting begins with a review of the legislation to be considered in the Parliament that week, and the decisions of the party executive on the attitude the party should take. Then, after questioning of the party leadership, the meeting considers any proposal by backbenchers of resolutions which they want to put on the parliamentary notice paper, including any private members' Bills which are proposed.

But unlike the Labor Caucus, the joint Liberal–National Party meeting is not held to make decisions about legislation or policies. It is for information and (occasionally) the letting off of steam—a safety valve for frustrated backbenchers. Votes are not taken as a matter of course, as in the Labor Caucus. And dissenting voices can be ignored by the party leadership (provided there is no suggestion that there might be a challenge launched against the leadership). In a coalition Government, the ultimate decision-making body is the Cabinet, not the party meeting. And yet, the strength of feeling in the party meeting can be (and has been in the past) such that the Cabinet has decided not to proceed with a piece of legislation it had previously authorised, or to change a policy, including a budget policy, which it had publicly announced. The power to discipline the leadership is the only power the Liberal Party meeting has, in theory, but in practice that power is sufficient to give it great influence on any matter on which there is strong party feeling. There may need to be more than the bare majority support, which in the Labor Party can result in a Cabinet decision being overturned, but there is no room for autocratic, one-man rule in the Liberal Party (as there may have been in times past).

Both the Liberal and National parties also hold separate party meetings, though these tend to be limited to domestic issues, such as the election of party delegates for trips or committees. The two parties also hold a separate meeting of their Senate parties, which is concerned essentially with the way in which they will treat Senate parliamentary business.

Very occasionally, however, the major parties will agree that a particular issue raises a matter of 'conscience' for individual MPs which makes it undesirable (and possibly dangerously impractical) for the party to try to exercise its normal discipline. Divorce law reform has been one such issue, abortion another. But, in a quite different vein, MPs are also normally given a 'free vote' on significant issues concerning Parliament and its procedure—such as the question of where the new Parliament House was to be built.

The smaller parties display a contrasting attitude to the notion of unity. The National Party is as dedicated as the Labor Party to maintaining a unified face, and is more successful in achieving it. On the other hand, the Australian Democrats glory in the fact that their parliamentary representatives do have some freedom to vote as they wish, and there have been occasions when the Democrats have split their vote in the Senate (for example, on retrospective tax legislation).

The Australian Democrats have sufficiently few Senators not only to make possible, but virtually to require, the fullest possible measure of party democracy. Strategy and tactics can all be decided on a daily basis by the whole of the party's parliamentary membership. Each of the Senators is responsible for shadowing a group of Ministers (each Senator has to try to be a specialist in five or six different departments) but decisions tend to be taken on a group basis, after research by staff and interested party members. The group is sufficiently small for all to be involved in decision-making. Individual Senators act as spokesmen or women, but few decisions need to be taken so urgently that the rest of the parliamentary members of the party cannot be consulted. The Senators do not have so many commitments elsewhere as to preclude them meeting every day to make collective decisions. But, despite the extensive consultation, the party also insists that its members are free to vote in Parliament as they see fit. Occasionally—more frequently than occurs with the Liberal Party which also proclaims the freedom of its MPs and Senators, the Australian Democrats will divide against each other in the Senate. But mostly the members of the party work out a common view and vote as a party.

Party committees

The major parties are too large and the time available in their meetings is too short for them to deliberate and decide on every matter that comes before the Parliament. As with the Parliament itself, the parliamentary parties have turned increasingly to the creation of committees for the detailed examination of policies and legislation. These committees are in a position to develop expertise in their own areas, and to have experts advise them on the implications and desirability of the proposals which are before them. They can be extremely influential in the development of policy, whether the party concerned is in Government or in Opposition. And in recent years party committees of the party in Government have been able to change proposed legislation— indeed some of the committees have had more effect on the final shape of proposed laws than the party as a whole or the Parliament as a whole.

The party committees have a comparatively recent history, at least in terms of the influence they are occasionally able to exercise. Liberal Party committees began developing in the late 1940s, when Sir Robert Menzies was the party's leader. But it was not until the mid-1970s, when Mr Malcolm Fraser became the Party's leader, that they began to exercise real influence, and to be able to make changes of substance to proposed Liberal legislation. It was during the 1970s that the party committee structure became quite formalised.

Until the 1970s the main function of the backbench Liberal committees was to serve as a means of providing information to MPs and Senators who would be expected to speak in a particular debate. They were usually informed of what the Government was about to do only shortly before the Government announced its plans publicly. While some of them attempted to develop policy and to influence Ministers and the Government, their achievements tended to be small. However, Prime Minister Fraser decided to increase the power of the committees. Firstly, he gave the committees power to review proposed legislation before it went into the party room. The Committees were able to propose amendments to Bills, to delete portions from them, and even, in extreme cases, to veto them altogether. Through their review of legislation, the committees kept Ministers on their toes. Ministers had to know what they were proposing, and what it meant, and not just accept what the public service may have put to them. The committees had access to senior public servants, but also to whomever else they chose to consult, and who was prepared to talk with them. This included industry leaders and representatives of industry (lobbyists). And the committees were not restricted to reviewing legislation which Ministers put to them—they could also initiate inquiries leading to the development of new policies or the review of existing ones.

As part of this system, a committee which consisted of the chairmen of the various committees was formed, essentially to create guidelines for the committees, and to co-ordinate the staffing of them (essentially, the provision of secretarial and some research assistance).

The Labor Party's party committees were in existence when the party was elected to Government in 1972. They had been reorganised over the preceding three years to allow for self-nomination (rather than election) to each committee, and to provide for unlimited membership—both processes adopted also by the Liberal–National Party committee system. Labor Ministers were required to submit all (except confidential) matters to the relevant committee before they went to Caucus or Cabinet. After discussion by the committee a legislative proposal would go to Cabinet and then to the Caucus where, if it had received committee endorsement, it would normally have no difficulties. Between 1972 and 1975 the scheme worked well with those Ministers who used it, and created tensions when Ministers tried to avoid their committees. The system was reorganised again in the mid-1970s, and was in place when the Labor Government was elected in 1983. Complaints about the lack of consultation between the Government and some of the committees led to further changes, not so much in the committees themselves as in the access provided between the committees and the Cabinet.

The committees are designed in such a way as to cover the whole range of Government activity, but both parties have chosen to have fewer committees than there are Ministers. There were eighteen Liberal–National Party committees at the beginning of 1985, including the committee of chairmen of committees. The Labor Party had fifteen committees, two of them described as co-ordinating committees, and one a liaison committee. There were twenty-seven Ministers, which these committees on both sides of the House were, in effect, shadowing. On both sides of politics, the committees combined Defence and Foreign Affairs into a single committee. Other committees tended to have functions which also cut across the boundaries of ministerial departments, involving most committees in the work of two or three different Ministers. Other committees looked at particular areas not related to the usual governmental structure—for example, the Labor Party had committees on Status of Women, and Youth Affairs.

Both parties allow MPs and Senators to be members of whichever committees they wish to join. However, Labor MPs and and Senators are only allowed to be members of a maximum of three committees. Liberal and National Party Ministers, unlike their Labor counterparts, are not allowed to be members of the committees. On both sides, the chairmen of the respective committees are elected by the committee members, and not appointed by the party leadership.

The committees, particularly those on the Government side, tend to be very busy during parliamentary sessions, each committee meeting on average for several hours each week. At those meetings, briefings may be provided by members of the committee, or by the staff of MPs or Ministers, or through papers prepared by the Parliamentary Library, or by public servants (who, under officially approved guidelines, are allowed to provide factual information for both Government and Opposition committees), or by people quite outside the parliamentary and governmental systems altogether, such as industry representatives or academics. The committees are not restricted in where or when they meet. When Parliament is in recess, they are just as likely to meet outside of Canberra. Because MPs and Senators have unlimited air travel throughout Australia, the meetings can be arranged at any place which is convenient for committee members. Members may wish to travel interstate to inspect particular industries or educational establishments, or to survey a particular region, or to interview a group of people they want information from.

As the committees and their work have become more widely known in recent years, they have become an important focus for people or organisations trying to feed information into the political policy-making process. Sometimes the committees seek out information from industry groups, or trade unions, or individuals; sometimes the information is offered to them (offers which are rarely declined). Sometimes the Parliamentary Library may be asked by both Opposition and Government committees to supply virtually the same information—the Library does not make public the requests for information which it gets, or make available the information it collates for one MP to any other, unless it has a specific request for the same kind of information. It is not unusual for Government and Opposition committees both to seek advice or information from a visiting overseas expert while he is in Canberra.

The power and influence of the committees vary greatly. Naturally, those of the Government party can have a more direct influence on the shape of legislation presented to the Parliament, and can influence Government policy as it is being formed and before it is put into effect. Opposition committees are restricted to helping to determine Opposition responses to Government legislation and to developing Opposition policies. But even so, this is a considerable change from the days when policies were essentially the prerogative of the party leadership, and the backbench had little opportunity to contribute until it was too late—until the policy had been fully developed, approved and announced.

But the impact of individual committees is likely to depend on the power of its chairman and his relationship with the Ministers or shadow Ministers whose portfolios come within the committee's ambit, and with the tasks which the committee sets itself and the quality of its work. Because many of the Labor committees were not having as much influence as they thought they should, the Labor Party revised its committee system early in 1985 to ensure that Cabinet was directly informed of committee views when it was considering significant issues. The party agreed that Ministers should initiate discussions with party committees on policy matters at the earliest possible stage; that except with highly sensitive matters, policy issues should be raised with committees before they were taken to Cabinet; that there should be continuous consultation between Ministers and committee chairmen about policy issues which might arise; that Cabinet should be informed in each Cabinet submission of what consultation had taken place in relation to that issue; and that Cabinet and its committees could hear or receive submissions from committee chairmen where there had not been sufficient consultation or where there was disagreement between the committee and the Minister. It also decided there should be regular reviews of the system by the Prime Minister and committee chairmen.

A new form of parliamentary democracy?

Party committees have enjoyed considerable popularity with backbenchers, all but a few of whom have voluntarily taken up committee posts. They undoubtedly affect the way in which legislation is handled both before and during its passage through the Parliament, and contribute to a greater understanding by MPs and Senators of the mass of material they process through the Parliament. There are critics of the development, however, who have suggested that its full implications for the parliamentary process have not been properly explored.

The first complaint is about the secrecy of the committees. All their operations are kept secret from the general public. No public indication is (usually) given of what the committees consider, decide or recommend, or of the effects of their recommendations. Parliamentarians have moved their primary examination of legislation from the floor of the House of Representatives and the Senate into committee rooms—and the committees which consider the proposed laws are not even committees of the Parliament, but party committees. In those committee rooms, representatives of industry, commerce, finance and the unions and pressure groups of all kinds can argue their point of view in secret, to the detriment of public debate. The process has also embroiled the public service which is supposed to provide advice only to Government. The public service is put at some risk of becoming involved in partisan party politics. A final criticism is that the minor parties are excluded altogether from this process. They simply cannot operate on a scale which matches the resources available to the major parties, which means that in the Parliament itself, minor party members are not likely to have access to the whole range of information which has been provided to members of the party committees of the major parties. A more general, and possibly more important, criticism is that the quite considerable time and effort devoted by backbenchers to the party committees is at the expense of their contribution to the Parliament itself.

The proponents of the system believe these possible disadvantages are outweighed by their advantages. The most important of these is the desirability of the way in which backbenchers have been drawn into the policy-making and legislative processes. The party committees result in a far wider range of MPs and Senators having an input into law making at a time when a proposed law is most able to be changed—before it is introduced into the Parliament (where it becomes more difficult to alter because of the way the media approach and report politics, characterising almost any changes to a Bill as being a 'defeat' for the Government). The access of people outside the Parliament to the party committees is also seen as a positive advantage, in that it provides more access by voters and interest groups to the Government and to parliamentarians, in a way which would not be possible if each MP was an isolated legislator, trying to gauge public opinion, or even expert opinion, for himself or herself.

Another advantage of the party committee system is that it reduces the isolation of Ministers. Backbenchers have long complained, under Governments of both political colours, that Ministers tend to lose contact with their parliamentary colleagues and with the people who elected them because they come to rely too much on the public servants who are their first source of advice. The party committee system increases contact in both directions. Ministers have to be less secretive about their plans (which means there is a chance for policies to be changed by party opinion before they are made public); and backbenchers are able to contribute their ideas and proposals on subjects which may be of concern in the community generally, but which have not otherwise been drawn to the attention of Ministers, or which Ministers may not have considered sufficiently important. The two-way communications opened up by the system mean that it is far more likely that the Government will work towards more consensus, at least within the ranks of its party members in the Parliament. It means that party differences, or differences between the parties in the coalition, can be worked out before matters go on public view.

The development of party committees can be seen as a response to a situation which had developed over a long period in which the party system and the media hardened the arteries of the Parliament's legislative system. The Commonwealth Parliament had long since ceased to play a full role in examining the details of legislation, or in seriously considering the merits of amendments, whether proposed by the Opposition or by backbenchers—in fact Government backbenchers in the House of Representatives had virtually ceased to propose amendments to Government legislation. Backbenchers are now back in the business of studying the laws they are making in the Parliament and trying to improve them, even though they are now doing so in party committees rather than in parliamentary committees or the Parliament itself. They are also in much greater contact with the community and with voters, not merely in the traditional ways (passing on complaints or representations from their constituents to Ministers or the public service) but by sitting on committees to examine the pros and cons of arguments in relation to specific policies or proposed laws. The backbenchers on the Opposition side have become more involved in policy making, while those on the Government side have become a part of the governmental process.

CHAPTER 9

A Parliamentarian's Parliamentary Day

When Parliament sits, the day takes on a quite different complexion for the Prime Minister and his Ministers, the Leader of the Opposition and his colleagues, and for the parliamentary office holders. In a sense, the parliamentary day ought to be the standard working day in the life of the people who are elected to Parliament. But Parliament only sits for about seventy days a year, and the working days of most parliamentarians are spent elsewhere. For Ministers, Parliament is a major distraction from the business of Government—though sometimes a pleasant distraction. For the Opposition, Parliament provides one of its best opportunities to make an impact in the national political scene, though it often turns out to be frustratingly difficult to get any attention at all.

The Prime Minister and his Ministers

The parliamentary day begins a long time before Parliament begins to sit. The daily diary of the Prime Minister or a Minister will normally begin with a long list of appointments involving governmental matters. There will be meetings with departmental officers to discuss particular items of policy which need to be reviewed, or which are about to be discussed with Cabinet or in Parliament, or which are on the agenda for future decision. There may be a briefing from a departmental officer about a speech the Minister is going to make, or a meeting he is to attend, or an interview he is about to give. There may be a formal meeting with one of the fifty or more ambassadors or diplomatic heads of mission who work in Canberra and who make the rounds of all Ministers who are in departments which determine matters of significance for their particular country—trade, primary industry, education, the environment, for example. Or there may be a meeting with a constituent, or a businessman or a lobbyist about some matter of departmental or government policy with which he is concerned. Such a meeting might have been arranged through a backbencher, or another Minister, or by the Minister's personal staff.

Among the more demanding pressures are those imposed by Press Gallery journalists seeking interviews, either on or off the record. It is rare that such meetings with the press are on the Minister's formal program. They mostly arise without any notice at all, as a result of political developments not of the Minister's making. A report in a morning newspaper about something concerning him or his portfolio may result in a Minister getting calls for more information or comment from radio and television as well as newspaper journalists. Some of these may be handled by his staff—by a press secretary or a private secretary handling press relations—but only the Minister can make a 'live' comment for a radio current affairs program, or be interviewed for television. Early morning television programs may require the Minister to be interviewed by 7.30 in the morning; radio interviewers may ring him even earlier, to record his comments over the telephone. Meetings with newspaper journalists are normally not so pressing. A journalist may want to talk about a current issue or about some new policy he believes the Minister or his Department or the Government is developing. He may want to be 'backgrounded' (receive information on a non-attributable basis) about views the Minister is rumoured to have expressed in Cabinet, or in Caucus. Or he may want an on-the-record interview for a feature in a magazine section.

Meetings of Cabinet, Cabinet committees and party committees will fill much of the day. The Caucus or coalition party meeting is held regularly on Tuesday mornings during parliamentary sittings weeks. Full Cabinet meetings are usually scheduled for times when the House of Representatives is not sitting—generally on Mondays. However, Cabinet committees and party committee meetings are regularly held during parliamentary sitting times and frequently have to be adjourned when a division or quorum is called and the MPs or Senators have to dash off to answer the insistent summons of the division bells. And it is not unusual for even a meeting of the full Cabinet to have to be held during sitting times and risk disruption through parliamentary demands.

Another regular feature of the daily parliamentary diary of the Prime Minister and most other Ministers is a pre-Question Time briefing, held for thirty to forty-five minutes immediately before Question Time. Each Minister holds a separate meeting with his own personal staff, sometimes with senior departmental staff in attendance, to prepare for what they all imagine could happen during Question Time. The Minister will have already read briefs prepared by his department on any current topic likely to be the subject of an Opposition question, and sought any supplementary information he thought necessary. The briefing session may review some of these matters, but it generally concentrates on the most significant political developments of the day, and reviews the likely way any particularly difficult questions might be answered. The briefing may also consider the placing of a question with a Government backbencher, to give the Minister an opportunity to reveal a new policy or to attack some aspect of Opposition policy which is in the news, or which he wants to turn to his political advantage.

Attendance at Question Time is virtually compulsory for the Prime Minister and all his Ministers, and being out of the country is about the only acceptable reason (other than illness) for being absent. If a Minister is in Australia he is expected to attend Parliament when it is sitting. If he cannot avoid an interstate appointment for reasons of urgency, he will still try to attend Question Time before flying off to his meeting.

Ministers in the House of Representatives have to spend comparatively little of the remainder of their working day actually in the House, though they do have to be on call for divisions at any hour of the parliamentary day. Ministers have to be in the House when any Bill for which they are responsible is being debated, though the Prime Minister and the Treasurer (who normally have other Ministers who assist them and to represent them in the House when their legislation is being discussed) are able to spend less time in the Chamber than other Ministers. Ministers are also expected to be present during important Government announcements, and during debates in which the Prime Minister is participating. Ministers are also 'rostered' to be present in the House at other periods to ensure that there is always a Minister able to take charge if the Opposition tries to change the planned program or tries to disrupt proceedings. Senate Ministers have a far more intensive parliamentary commitment. Because there are so few of them (in recent years, normally five or six) and because there has to be a Minister in the Senate in charge of the Government's interest all the time, each Minister is likely to spend at least an hour or two a day in addition to Question Time, in the Senate Chamber. Each Senate Minister also has to 'shadow' a series of House of Representatives Ministers, answering questions about their portfolios as well as the Minister's own. When acting as a representative of another Minister, a Senate Minister has to try to ensure that there is not an Opposition trap, designed to get different answers to the same question being asked at the same time in the two Chambers.

Ministers are not completely tied down at their Parliament House offices when Parliament is sitting. It is generally possible for a Minister to be able to arrange a pair with an Opposition member to be absent for a few hours to attend a dinner being held by a national industry group, or a meeting being conducted by a union, or to open a meeting, or launch a book, or dedicate some monument or trophy. Ministers also get regular invitations to diplomatic functions, and to Government House when the Governor-General is hosting a dinner for some visiting dignitary.

The Opposition leadership

The Opposition Leader and his shadow ministry do not have anywhere near the parliamentary constraints on their time that are suffered by Ministers. In one sense it is the Opposition which calls the parliamentary tune. It is the Opposition which decides when there should be a censure motion, when it will go on the attack, when it will call quorums or divisions or propose amendments, and when it will try to disrupt the regular flow of parliamentary business. Opposition members do not have to answer quorum calls—though it is they who call quorums hoping to catch out the Government and embarrass it. The Opposition leadership is not required to attend Question Time, or any other parliamentary activity (though attendance at Question Time is normally very good). It is far easier for an Opposition shadow Minister to arrange to attend a meeting interstate, or talk to a group in Canberra away from Parliament House, than it is for a Minister. The main consideration for the Opposition is the political impact it can make through attacking the Government in several places at the one time—outside as well as inside Parliament. Convention requires the Government to concentrate its forces on the parliamentary arena.

In fact the Opposition Leader and his most senior colleagues do have a round of meetings and interviews during the parliamentary day which is quite comparable to that of many Ministers, though of course they are not involved in decision making affecting the conduct of Government.

The Opposition shadow ministry normally meets on the first Monday of a parliamentary sitting fortnight to plan its general tactics for those sitting days, and to decide what attitudes it will adopt to the various proposed laws the Government has introduced into the Parliament. Its decisions (recommendations in the case of a Labor shadow ministry) will be based on recommendations of the shadow Minister responsible for handling each particular matter, and on any consideration of those recommendations by a party committee. Normally, both the shadow Minister and his committee will have spent some hours preparing their recommendations, and committees do not feel bound to accept the recommendations provided by shadow Ministers. The Opposition executive's decisions go to a party meeting the following day—for information in the case of the Liberal and National Party, for ratification in the case of the Labor Party.

The Opposition Leader holds an Opposition equivalent of a Minister's pre-Question Time briefing on each sitting day. He and his senior Opposition leaders, together with their senior staff, decide what the major thrust of the Opposition's questions should be for that day, and on any other parliamentary tactics. During the day the Opposition Leader will see in his rooms the same kind of people who visit Ministers—and often the very same people. Industry leaders, lobbyists, diplomats and overseas dignitaries will all want to pay calls on the Opposition as well as the Government. Sometimes their chances of getting what they want will be improved if the Opposition takes up their case. And most find it important to keep the Opposition informed in any event—Oppositions may be turned by elections into Governments, and people who want to do business with Governments have to look ahead to possible changes in the political scene. The Opposition Leader also has regular briefings on security matters from the intelligence and defence organisations.

Liberal Opposition leaders also have a more difficult time with their party meetings than do Labor leaders. The Labor Party leader does not have to act as chairman of the Caucus, but the Liberal leader not only has to preside at meetings of his party, but also to guide and end discussions without the benefit of any votes. He has to try to ease his way past difficult problems, and difficult backbenchers, without infuriating people in the party who disagree with decisions he has made.

The Opposition's shadow Ministers are kept busy with rounds of party committee meetings both to respond to what the Government is doing, and to prepare Opposition policy initiatives. But they are far less busy than the average Minister. Yet they have one task which Ministers generally manage to avoid—they normally have to prepare their own parliamentary speeches. Those speeches, on Matters of Public Importance, and giving the main response to Bills introduced by the Government, warrant a good deal of work, because as well as presenting a view on behalf of the Opposition, they are the individual shadow Minister's best opportunity to impress his colleagues with his public abilities.

Backbenchers

Backbenchers on both sides of the Parliament lead a quite different sort of parliamentary life from that of their more illustrious and famous colleagues on the Government or Opposition front bench. They too, tend to spend more time outside the parliamentary chamber than within it. But their non-parliamentary time is mostly spent in quite different ways. They tend to be particularly concerned about what is happening 'back home' in their electorates and with the continuous representations made to them by their electors. Most are also heavily involved with the work of the parliamentary committees and party committees of which they are members. They also have to devote some of their time to preparing to make their generally unpublicised contributions to the parliamentary process—their speeches in the House or the Senate on innumerable pieces of Government legislation.

In order to maximise the time that Ministers and backbenchers have available, most party committees meet during the lunch or dinner break and then continue during the time Parliament is sitting. Most backbenchers will attend two or three such meetings every week the Parliament is sitting. Some will also be on parliamentary committees which will meet on parliamentary days, but generally outside parliamentary sitting times. These meetings sometimes require considerable preparation by the backbencher, which he generally will have to do by himself, though sometimes with the aid of a research assistant on his staff and/or the parliamentary library.

Backbenchers do not have the array of visitors who call on Ministers or Opposition leaders, but they frequently have constituents call on them, seeking their aid in getting Government assistance or overcoming a Government decision. Those whose electorates are comparatively close to Canberra may also find that a party of schoolchildren from their electorate is planning a visit to Parliament House, a visit which often results in the MP providing a special afternoon tea for the visitors, or at least a good deal of his time in escorting them around and answering their questions.

As for Parliament itself, the backbencher has two main duties: he has to be available during divisions, to ensure that his party has the maximum vote possible; and he has to be willing to participate in debates when his whips call on his services. He may want to do many other things. He will certainly want to participate in Question Time if he can, though if he is a Member of the House of Representatives, time and other limitations will probably prevent him from asking a question more than about once every three sitting weeks—Senators are able to get a question almost every day. He will also want to speak in debates in any area where he has developed an expertise, or wants to publicly demonstrate an interest, such as on a subject which particularly concerns his electorate (for example, the car industry if he represents an area which has one of the car manufacturing plants, or the dairy industry if he is from a rural electorate where there are a substantial number of milk or cheese producers). He may want to speak on a subject to enhance his chances of joining a particular parliamentary committee, or of getting a Parliament-sponsored trip. Or he may wish to put the views of a constituent. But sometimes he may be asked to speak simply because the other side has a lot of speakers lined up and his own side has run out of people who want to speak on the particular subject.

Much of the backbencher's time, however, will be spent on electorate business. He is likely to be in touch with his secretary in his electorate several times during the day, and to spend a considerable amount of time dealing with correspondence from people who live in his electorate who have problems they want him to solve, or representations they want him to make. In marginal city electorates, a backbencher is likely to be contacted in one way or another by three or four thousand of his electors each year, and while many of their problems can be handled by his staff, his own intervention is frequently required. That may involve him talking to the person seeking his help, or to a Minister or a department. And if that has to be done in Canberra, it will generally be done on a parliamentary day.

In his spare time, the backbencher will try to catch up with the vast amount of reading provided for him by the Parliament and the Government. Hundreds of reports are tabled in the Parliament each year—far too many for any individual to read. The backbencher has to choose those which are of interest to him, or which are likely to be considered by any of the committees to which he belongs. There are also copies of press releases by Ministers, official government statistics, and parliamentary papers. Most of the committees also generate vast amounts of paper to be read— briefing papers prepared by staff or the library, or submissions by witnesses who want to give evidence, or draft questions or issues or reports. There may also be material which the library has prepared at his request to help in a speech he is going to make, or a submission he wants to prepare for a committee or a Minister or to help a constituent. And when he makes a speech or asks a question in the Parliament, he will have to revise a copy of the *Hansard* report of the speech, to ensure that what is reported is what he was trying to say.

Whatever the backbencher is doing, however, he will be within hearing of the bells which are installed in every office, corridor and public area, in the library, refreshment rooms and bars, in Ministers' offices and in the Cabinet room. The bells sound whenever there is a division in either House of Parliament. And a red or a green flashing light indicates whether the call is for the Senate or the House of Representatives. In his office, the MP or Senator will also have a loudspeaker which will be relaying the proceedings in the two Houses (a switch enables him to choose which to listen to, but almost invariably it will be tuned to his own House so that almost subconsciously he is aware of what is happening). If he happens to be in the Whips' office, or in the office of his Leader of the House, he can even see what is happening on closed-circuit television. And wherever he goes in the Parliament building, he will be expected to carry a pager, which can be dialled by his Whips, or through the internal telephone system. The average backbencher is required to be ready at all times to supply his vote and his services.

Life is different again for the Senator who is a member of a smaller party or who is an Independent. He or she is much more involved in decision making than the average backbencher. The Independent does not have to worry about party meetings, but he has a large number of people who want to see him to try to influence his vote because that vote could be important in a closely divided Senate. The member of the small party does have party meetings to worry about, but these meetings will cover tactics and strategy as well as responses to government legislation. Representatives of the smaller parties in the Parliament also have to consider the needs of their party organisation outside the Parliament. Normally the party cannot provide them with the back-up which the major parties receive. Indeed it is the parliamentary members of the minor parties who provide secretarial and other services (funded by the taxpayer) to help the outside party. Minor party members have to ensure that their parliamentary contributions make an impact—they cannot rely on anyone else to do it for them.

CHAPTER 10

Law Making

Parliament's primary function is to make laws. It raises taxation for the Government by passing laws and it passes laws to allow the Government to spend money. The laws passed by the Parliament determine what actions should be regarded as crimes and what the penalties should be when anyone breaks those laws. Some of the laws which the Parliament makes are used by public servants to decide such things as who gets what pensions, which schools get Commonwealth financial grants, and how many students should be admitted to universities and colleges. The Commonwealth Parliament makes the laws which govern marriage and divorce, immigration and citizenship. It establishes the rules under which banks and insurance companies operate. Its laws ban various kinds of restrictive trade practices and provide some protection for consumers. The Parliament's laws give the Government power to decide whether bans or restrictions should be put on any imports or exports.

Making those laws—several hundred each year—is a complex business. Parliamentary tradition has made the process seem more complex by making it a ritual with its own language. And the Australian Constitution has provided further difficulties by preventing the Commonwealth Parliament from making any laws in some areas, or by requiring it to observe special procedures in others.

Yet what happens in Parliament when it makes laws is very much a tip-of-the-iceberg phenomenon. Most of the work in preparing, amending and finalising the shape of the laws is done behind the scenes by public servants, by parliamentary draftsmen, by Ministers and the Cabinet, and, as noted in Chapter 8, by party committees—well before Parliament gets a look at the proposals.

But Parliament still has to give its approval before they become law.

Terminology

When the Parliament (which, according to the Constitution, means the Senate, the House of Representatives and the Queen) passes a law, it does so in the form of an Act of Parliament. An Act generally has a short title (e.g. *Customs Administration Act 1985*) by which it is officially known, and a long title (e.g. *An Act to establish an Australian Customs Service, and for purposes connected therewith*). It consists of a series of 'sections' which, as well as detailing the contents of the law, may also say when it takes effect, and what relationship its provisions have with existing laws. When the proposed law is introduced into Parliament, it is called A Bill for an Act to (e.g. establish an Australian Customs Service, and for purposes connected therewith), or more briefly, the Customs Administration Bill 1985. Its numbered paragraphs, which later are called sections, are referred to as 'clauses' while it is going through the parliamentary process. Following ancient (British) tradition, each Bill is given three 'readings' in each House of the Parliament. Most Bills are first introduced into the House of Representatives by a Minister, who the previous day has given 'notice' of the proposed Bill. He does this by giving a signed notice to the Clerk of the House, who reads it to the House during any break in the proceedings, saying simply, 'The Minister for Trade, has given notice that on the next day of sitting, he will introduce a Customs Administration Bill'. The next day the formal Notice Paper, which lists all the possible business for the House, will contain the name of the Bill, along with any others of which notice has been given, under the heading, Notices of Motion. At the time chosen by the Government for the introduction of Bills, the Minister is called on by the Speaker, and the Minister hands to the Clerk three printed copies of the Bill, and says, 'I present the Customs Administration Bill 1985'. The Clerk then stands and reads out the long title of the Bill, preceding this with the words:'First reading. A Bill for an Act to establish an Australian Customs Service and for purposes connected therewith'. There is no formal proposal that the House should vote on whether there should be a first reading, and no vote at that stage. The Minister then proceeds immediately with the second step in the process. He says,'I move that this Bill be now read a second time'. He then launches into his prepared speech which explains what the Bill is about, and why the Parliament should agree to it. At the same time, attendants will be moving around the Chamber handing out copies of the Bill and, if it is at all complex, as it usually is, copies of what is officially called an 'explanatory memorandum', prepared by the Minister's Department, which goes through the Bill, clause by clause, explaining the meaning of each provision, and what it is intended to achieve. When the Minister finishes speaking, a member of the Opposition, usually the frontbencher 'shadowing' the Minister, moves the adjournment of the debate, and this automatically occurs. The debate is not normally taken up in the House again for at least a week, during which time the Opposition has a chance to study it (in its relevant party committee) and decide whether it is going to support the Bill, oppose it, or try to have it changed.

At a time agreed by the Government and Opposition, the Bill is relisted for debate, the Clerk tells everyone what is to be debated ('Order of the Day number 5. Customs Administration Bill, resumed debate on the second reading') and the shadow Minister makes his second reading speech outlining the attitude to be taken by the Opposition. If the Opposition is completely or partly opposed to the Bill, he will sometimes move an amendment which is in the form: 'That all words after "that" be deleted and the following be put in their place: That the House declines to give the Bill a second reading because (or, that the Bill should be redrafted to take account of. . .' The somewhat strange beginning of this amendment is a reference to the strict terms of the motion that the House is debating, which is 'That the Bill be read a second time'! After the shadow Minister's speech, the House immediately proceeds with a full-scale debate on the merits of the Bill and any Opposition amendment. The debate may last only briefly if the Bill is not controversial, or there may be so many MPs wanting to speak that the debate has to be carried over to the next day (or, more rarely for several days). At the end of the debate a vote is taken on the amendment and the motion for the second reading. When that is carried the Clerk again stands in his place and formally reads the long title of the Bill again.

The next stage is supposed to be the 'committee' stage of the Bill. The Bill is meant to be considered in detail, possibly on a clause-by-clause basis. But this only occurs in the House to about a quarter or a fifth of the Bills, when there are specific changes to the Bill which the Opposition wants to propose (rather than the grander condemnation it might have moved at the second reading stage). Occasionally the Government itself may want to move amendments to its own Bill, to pick up and meet criticisms which have been made by either its own supporters or the Opposition, or to correct errors which have been discovered. After the Clerk has read the Bill a second time, the Speaker will ask 'Is it the desire of the House to proceed with the third reading forthwith?'. If it is not (that is, if there are amendments which do have to be discussed and determined) the House then moves 'into committee'.

The committee is actually the whole of the membership of the House but in exceptional circumstances the Bill can be referred to a special legislative committee to examine the Bill in great detail, possibly using witnesses to advise on the merits of particular parts of the Bill. The House created some such legislative committees between 1978 and 1982 but they functioned little then, and have not since been used. The Senate has standing committees which it does use for examining legislation occasionally. The House signifies its move 'into committee' in a number of ways. The Speaker leaves his Chair, and the Chairman of Committees (the Deputy Speaker) moves into a chair between the two Clerks, and directly below the Speaker's Chair. At the same time the Serjeant-at-Arms removes the mace from the end of the central table and places it out of view in a special bracket on the end of the table. All this means that the House of Representatives as such is not sitting, but has been replaced by a committee of the House.

In Committee, the House proceeds to a clause-by-clause study of the Bill, skipping quickly through those parts which are not to be debated, or to which amendments will not be moved. The Chairman will put it 'that clauses 1 to 8 be agreed to' before calling for the debate on clause 9, for example. After the whole of the Bill has been considered the committee gives way to the meeting of the whole House again, with the Speaker moving back into his place, and the mace being replaced. The chairman of committees reports that the Bill has been agreed to, with or without amendments, the House adopts the committee's report, and the Minister then moves that the 'Bill be read a third time', which is usually agreed to without a vote. The Clerk completes the formalities by reading the Bill's title for the third time.

The Bill then is taken over to the Senate, where the same kind of formalities are observed: three readings including a committee stage, which, unlike the House, the Senate does persist with. The same debating is done and in the case of the Minister introducing the Bill, generally the same speech is made as was made in the House (in fact, it is often simply incorporated in *Hansard* without the Senate Minister having to read it). There are some slight variations in procedure (there is a vote on the first reading, for example) and some of the motions are phrased slightly differently. There are fewer short-cuts than are adopted in the House.

If the Senate passes amendments to a Bill which was sent to it by the House of Representatives, it sends a message to the House listing those amendments. The message is then considered by the House 'in committee'. The two Houses can exchange messages about the nature of any amendments until they reach agreement, or until it is clear that there is a total disagreement. If the two Houses cannot agree on the final form of the Bill, it has no effect. The Government may try to introduce it three months later and argue that any refusal by the Senate to pass it would mean that the grounds would exist for a 'double dissolution' of both Houses of the Parliament. The Senate may nevertheless continue with its Opposition to the Bill, and risk the political consequences (or call the Government's bluff, if that is what it thinks it is).

After passing both Houses, a Bill is sent to the Governor-General who signs it in order to give it the 'Royal assent'. The Bill is then an Act, and has the full force of law, unless it contains a clause which provides that it is to come into effect at some specified time (say, 1 January the following year), or at a time to be 'proclaimed'—by a notice published in the *Commonwealth Gazette* given by the Governor-General at the request of the Minister responsible for the administration of the Act.

Not all Bills are dealt with by the Parliament precisely in this way. Special procedures have to be adopted in particular for financial Bills (in fact, there are a whole series of special terms which are used to describe various types of Bills—money Bills, tax Bills, Appropriation Bills, Supply Bills. There are special provisions in the Constitution about most of these types of Bills, and special measures adopted, particularly in the Senate, when they are being considered by the Parliament.

One important constitutional requirement seems to limit the Senate's power. Section 53 of the Constitution says that the 'Senate may not amend proposed laws imposing taxation, or proposed laws appropriating revenue or moneys for the ordinary annual services of the Government'. However the same section does permit the Senate to make 'requests' of the House of Representatives, and these requests are effectively the same as amendments, particularly as the Senate usually makes sure that it does not give the third reading to a Bill to which it is requesting changes, until it has had a positive response to its request.

Section 53 of the Constitution also prohibits the Senate from amending any proposed law so as 'to increase any proposed charge or burden on the people'. It also requires proposed laws appropriating revenue or moneys, or imposing taxation to originate in the House of Representatives and not the Senate.

Other constitutional provisions require the separation of the various forms of taxation into different Bills, so that each deals with only one kind of tax. Customs laws can deal only with customs duties and laws about excise duties cannot deal with any other subject. These requirements (and related ones) result in a great many different Bills having to be put to the Parliament to deal with one general subject. For example, half a dozen different Acts of Parliament may be needed to put into effect a primary industry marketing scheme, in which growers are taxed to contribute towards a stabilisation scheme and to provide funds for industry research funds. Parliament tends to deal with such Bills in a group, having what it calls a 'cognate' debate on a series of Bills on a related subject.

Governments cannot raise money (through taxes, customs or excise, or in any other way, such as by charges for services, or fees, or stamp duties) unless they have parliamentary approval. They also cannot spend money from what they have collected without a separate set of Acts of Parliament. The Constitution also requires that the Parliament cannot pass Acts to spend ('appropriate') money, without a 'recommendation' from the Governor-General to that effect. Of course the Governor-General makes such recommendations when asked to by the Government. Much of the money-raising and spending legislation is concentrated into what has become known as the Budget session of Parliament. On Budget night the Treasurer introduces a series of Bills—two Appropriation Bills, the first covering the 'ordinary annual expenses' of Government, and the second containing expenses on capital items—buildings, grants to organisations, and other items not concerned with the actual running of the public service. There are generally Tax Bills changing rates of taxation in some way, customs and excise Bills to alter taxes on petrol or cigarettes, sales tax Bills, customs tariff Bills (if rates of duty on some imports are to be changed), bounty Bills, to provide any assistance which the Government has decided to give to manufacturing industry and a loan Bill to authorise the Government to borrow money. In 1984, for example, there were ten Bills introduced during the week in which the Budget was presented to carry out the financial policy announced in the Budget. Other Bills related to the Budget include States Grants Bills, which set the conditions under which the Commonwealth gives the States money for such things as roads, education and health.

The Treasurer makes his Budget speech in the form of a second reading speech to the first of the Budget Bills, the Appropriation Bill No. 1. And the rest of the debate in the House on the Budget, which can occupy the next two months, also, formally, is on that Bill. At the end of the debate, all the Budget Bills are processed very quickly through the House. The Senate adopts a realistic, if somewhat unusual, approach to the Budget. The Minister representing the Treasurer in the Senate reads the Budget speech there, though not as a 'second reading' speech. And then the specially-created Senate estimate committees begin an exhaustive study of all of the estimates which are attached to the Appropriation Bill—the Bill itself is only a few paragraphs long, but attached to it are a few hundred pages detailing the way thousands of millions of dollars are expected to be spent. The estimates committees generally finish their work about the time the House of Representatives votes on the Budget and sends it to the Senate.

The Senate estimates committees conduct a similar but less intensive exercise in the first half of the year, when the Government introduces two more Appropriation Bills (Nos 3 and 4) to cover additional expenditures not anticipated when the Budget was introduced in August. At the same time the Government introduces what are called Supply Bills—Bills which provide for Government expenditure in the first five months of the next financial year—July to the end of November . This is needed because the Budget Bills are not generally passed until about the end of November, five months after the beginning of the financial year. Because the Supply Bills are supposed to be just an interim measure to keep the Government in funds until the true Budget Bills are passed, they do not contain any new measures. The amounts they provide are simply calculated on the basis of the previous year's Budget allocations. Because they are supposed to last just five months, they simply contain 5/12ths of the amounts provided for the Government in the previous twelve months.

The Appropriation Bills contain items about virtually every facet of Government, and as a result, debates about the merits of passing the Bills can extend over every activity of Government, and not be restricted just to the economic policies of the Government. In debating other Bills, MPs and Senators have to keep fairly closely to the subject of the particular piece of proposed legislation—they cannot just get on their feet and talk about anything under the sun (there are special occasions for wide-ranging debates). The Senate provides a further opportunity for general debates in any 'money' Bill which is sent to it by the House of Representatives. Senators are allowed to debate the first reading (which is never debated or even voted on in the House) and can talk about anything in first reading debates on Bills which the Senate is barred, by the Constitution, from amending.

The legislative program

Parliament has a great deal of regular legislation for its consideration—the Budget and the various financial Bills throughout the year, States grants Bills and several Bills in which minor amendments to existing legislation is collected. The content of this legislation varies from year to year, but in some form or another it is always on the program. In addition, Governments know that there is always a good deal of administrative legislation necessary to put to Parliament—Bills to tidy up or change procedures used by the public service in the administration of health services or social security or the management of the defence forces. There are two other major types of legislation for which space has to be found on the Parliamentary program. The first relates to policy initiatives—Bills putting into effect promises made by the Government at election time or policies later adopted by the Government. The other is urgent unforeseen Bills, which are needed to implement an international treaty, or deal with a crisis in federal–state relations, or repair a legal loophole which has been exposed by the courts. All these pieces of legislation have to be drafted, approved by the Cabinet and the governing parliamentary party and its committees, and then given to the Parliament for its consideration. The amount of time and resources available to both the Government and the Parliament are limited, and at the beginning of each parliamentary session the Government has to determine its legislative priorities. In recent years the Leader of the House has, towards the beginning of each session, given the Parliament an outline of the main proposals the Government hopes to put to the Parliament in the next few months.

The planning process begins with Ministers putting in bids for spaces on the legislative program for legislation in which they or their departments have a particular demand. Priorities are determined by a parliamentary business committee of Cabinet and the Prime Minister, which determines whether proposals should be included on a list of Bills which must or should be passed in the coming session, or a list of those which should be proceeded with if there is time, or a list of Bills which are to be introduced into the Parliament but not passed until a later session. Normally the committee has to reduce the list by a third to a half, to keep the workload for the parliamentary draftsmen and for the Parliament at a manageable level. The draftsmen begin working on the proposed Bills in accordance with the priorities determined by the committee. Before that stage is reached, however, the policy issues involved have to be settled by the Minister and the relevant party committee, and a Cabinet submission on the need for the legislation and outlining its major contents processed through Cabinet and its committees. Once drafted, the Bill has to be reconsidered by the party committee and by the Legislation Committee of the Cabinet, to ensure that it complies with the guidelines approved by the Cabinet. It then has to be finally approved by the parliamentary party, before it is put on the schedule of Bills for introduction into the House or Senate.

Sometimes the whole process can be greatly reduced, when urgent legislation is needed to meet a crisis. But urgent Bills hold up the consideration by the Parliament of the regularly scheduled Bills.

No matter what planning is done, however, the Parliament almost invariably faces a major legislative squeeze towards the end of each session. Governments normally have to gag or guillotine Bills through the House of Representatives in its last sitting week, and the Senate sits for an additional week to clear up the last legislation passed on to it by the House. This 'legislation by exhaustion' as it is inevitably called by the Opposition of the day sometimes involves extremely important legislation. Governments are accused of using the press of business to prevent full and proper discussion of important legislation. But when Oppositions become Governments after elections, they too find themselves using 'legislation by exhaustion' to push through the last of each session's legislative program.

Subordinate (or delegated) legislation

The legislation actually passed by Parliament, in the form of Acts of Parliament, is only about half of the law making actually carried out by the Commonwealth and its various authorities during a year. But all of that additional law making is done with the permission and approval of the Parliament under various Acts of the Parliament and can be reviewed and, if necessary, rejected by the Parliament. These additional laws, often referred to as subordinate legislation, go by a variety of names—such as regulations, ordinances and statutory rules (including rules made by various courts), by-laws, determinations and orders.

They are subordinate (in the sense of secondary, or subject to a superior) because they depend for their effect on something already decided by Parliament. Many Acts of Parliament specifically provide that various parts of the law making process will be carried out through the making of regulations. The aim is that the Act of Parliament will set down the general principles but that details, particularly minor details which might be changed fairly frequently, should be dealt with by regulations. The regulations cannot be at odds with the original Act—in fact the Act will generally specify the areas in which regulations can be made in and the kind of material they should specify. The matters which are intended to be included in regulations rather than in the original legislation are such things as the fees to be paid for various services provided by Government Departments and authorities, the forms which need to be filled in to obtain services or information, addresses where applications have to be lodged, and the times within which various procedures have to be taken. But if the regulation-making power in a particular law is wide enough, regulations can be used for extensive law making. The Senate Regulations and Ordinances Committee examines all subordinate legislation to see whether it intrudes on civil liberties (see Chapter 7) and draws the Senate's attention to any subordinate legislation which it considers should be changed or rejected.

The common feature of all the subordinate legislation is that it is capable of being reviewed by the Parliament—in fact by either of the Houses of Parliament. Under the Acts Interpretation Act, all subordinate legislation is required to be laid before both Houses of the Parliament. Within fifteen sitting days, either House can then pass a motion disallowing any regulation or ordinance or other piece of subordinate legislation. The House or the Senate cannot change any of the regulations or other subordinate legislation but its power to reject them altogether provides it with a means of persuading responsible Ministers or departments to make required changes. If the changed are not made, the risk is that the regulations will be completely vetoed.

Parliamentary privilege

The Commonwealth Parliament (and the State Parliaments) inherited from Britain the notion that Members of Parliament needed to be protected, by the Parliament itself, from any 'outside' interference. The British Parliament was concerned to protect its Members from being prevented from attending to their parliamentary roles. The British Parliament was able to call on very special powers to achieve that aim. The original Parliament in mediaeval days (consisting of just one House of Parliament) had been recognised as the High Court of Parliament—it could make and unmake laws and decide what its own special rights and privileges were. When the Commons formed a separate House, they took some time to establish their own rights and privileges. It was not until the early 15th century that the Commons achieved any real power to enforce its will directly (through the use of a Royal Serjeant-at-Arms). More than a century later (in 1543), the Commons used their Serjeant to oppose the City of London and forced it to release one of its Members from prison, where he had been sent and held by the authority of the City of London. This action established the first of the defined 'privileges' of Parliament— freedom from arrest in civil cases. Over the centuries the Commons built up a series of such privileges, as well as a general power to punish anyone for 'contempt' of the Parliament.

When the Australian Parliament was created, the writers of the Constitution did not attempt to spell out the various privileges and powers of the individual Houses of Parliament. Instead they provided, in Section 49 of the Constitution, that:

> The powers, privileges, and immunities of the Senate and of the House of Representatives, and of the Members and the Committees of each House, shall be such as are declared by the Parliament, and until declared shall be those of the Commons House of Parliament of the United Kingdom, and of its Members and Committees, at the establishment of the Commonwealth.

Because the Australian Parliament has not made a general declaration (in the form of a law) about its 'powers, privileges and immunities' (though it has passed a few special laws dealing with a few of those powers: e.g., extending privilege against defamation actions for anything which is broadcast from Parliament on the ABC), the general law in relation to privileges remains what it was in Britain for the House of Commons in 1901, when the Commonwealth was formally established. This means that the law is slightly unclear and not always appropriate, in terms of the institutions dealt with by the law, and in terms of modern day life. One privilege belonging to Members of the House of Commons, for example, is freedom from appointment as a sheriff, a position which simply does not exist (other than in the court system) in Australia.

Serjeant-at-Arms

The privileges which are relevant, and have been carried over into the Australian Parliament, are:
- freedom of speech
- freedom from arrest in civil suits
- exemption from service as jurors
- exemption from attendance as witnesses.

Freedom of speech means freedom in Parliament. This is one of the very ancient privileges of MPs, and it was put in specific form in the Bill of Rights in 1689, which provided

> That the freedom of speech and debate or proceedings in Parliament ought not to be impeached or questioned in any court or place out of Parliament.

It means that MPs can say anything about anyone—subject to Parliament's own rules of debate, which prevent MPs and Senators from reflecting on the Queen, or her representatives, or using offensive words against either House of Parliament, or any MP or Senator, or any member of the judiciary.

Members may not be brought before the courts for anything they say in Parliament, which means that the ordinary laws of defamation simply do not apply to speeches in Parliament. The only body which can deal with Members for what they say in Parliament, is the Parliament itself. It is only likely to act if it thinks a Member has abused his privilege. There is a form of privilege which applies also to reports of what is said in Parliament. So long as what is reported is a fair report of what has been said in Parliament, it too is privileged, and the person, or newspaper or television station who tells others of what has been said in Parliament, is also able to do so without legal consequences. It may be that what an MP says or writes while he is looking after the interests of the people who live in his electorate, or what he does on other parliamentary business away from the Parliament, is also protected by this right to freedom of speech.

The justification for this privilege (as for almost all the others) is that without this freedom an MP cannot do his job properly. He has to be free to say what he thinks, without worrying about the consequences, if he is to do his job as a lawmaker and guardian of the public interest.

The second listed privilege, that against arrest in civil causes, is hardly relevant these days. The main civil cause for which people used to be arrested was debt. This 'remedy' has virtually been replaced by the bankruptcy laws. There are now so few occasions on which a person can be sent to gaol through a civil action brought by another person, that the privilege is almost meaningless. There are some actions, however, which Governments can instigate which may be classified as civil rather than criminal and which can result in imprisonment.

The third privilege, exemption from jury service, has been caught up in general provisions in the law, which provide exemption from jury service for many categories of people, including MPs and Senators.

The fourth privilege, from attendance as a witness, applies to both criminal and civil cases. The first duty of MPs is to attend the Parliament when it is sitting, and this cannot be overriden by a requirement by a Court that the MP should attend to give evidence. When Parliament is sitting, the courts normally excuse MPs from attending Court to give evidence, so that direct conflict does not arise.

Contempt of Parliament

These privileges belong to each and every member of the Parliament, and would normally be protected by the law of the land without any intervention by the Parliament. (The courts, for example, would recognise an MP's privilege of free speech in the Parliament if any defamation action was brought against the MP for something he had said in the Parliament.) But a series of other privileges or rights belong not to individual MPs but to the House of which he or she is a Member. A breach of any of these collective privileges or rights is said to be a contempt of Parliament. And some contempts go beyond breaches of specific privileges. Exactly what is a contempt in any circumstance is decided by the Parliament, and its decision cannot be overturned by any Court.

Some of these rights or privileges of the whole House (or Senate) are:

- the right to have the attendance of its Members
- the right to regulate its own internal affairs and procedures, free from interference from the courts
- the right to govern its own membership (subject to the Constitution), including the power to expel Members it finds guilty of disgraceful and infamous conduct
- the right to hold inquiries and to require the attendance of witnesses and the production of documents
- the right to administer oaths to witnesses
- the right to punish by committal (to prison) persons guilty of breaches of its privileges or other contempts

• the right to publish papers containing defamatory material.
One 'right' belonging to the House of Commons which was probably not given to the Australian Parliament was the House of Commons' ability to impeach—to put on trial a person (anyone from the monarch down) for treason or other high crime or misdemeanour beyond the reach of the law, or which no other authority would prosecute. The House of Commons by its vote puts the charge against the person, who is then tried by the House of Lords. Such a procedure is simply not envisaged by the Australian Constitution, which invests the 'judicial power of the Commonwealth' in the High Court and other federal courts.

The general contempt power (other than in relation to specific powers or privileges) is simply Parliament's power to protect its own workings. It is a protective power very similar to that used by the higher courts to protect themselves against disruption or attack. It covers any action (or lack of action) which obstructs or impedes either House in the performance of its functions, or which obstructs or impedes any Member of a House, or any official of the House in performing his duties—or even any action which just might produce such an obstruction. It does not matter that no one else has committed that kind of offence before. It is not the specific action which is a contempt, but the general activity of preventing or obstructing the House.

Using the privileges power

Complaints about breaches of privilege or contempt are usually raised by MPs or Senators, or, more rarely, are brought to the attention of the House or Senate by its presiding officer. The Parliament deals with about one complaint a year, on average. Most do not go much further than the complaint stage, being found, on investigation, not to raise a true point of privilege or contempt, or not to raise one of any significance. But if a Privileges Committee in either House finds, after investigation, that there has been a contempt, it reports its findings back to the House, which then has to decide what action it will take. The range of actions which is open to the Houses is fairly limited. The House can censure the person responsible (usually a newspaper which has printed something derogatory about the House or its Members) and demand an apology to be delivered in person at the bar of the House, or through a printed apology in a newspaper. It can also remove the journalists representing the offending paper from Parliament House for as long as it thinks appropriate. The most substantial penalty it can impose is a gaol sentence—an action taken by the House of Representatives just once, when in 1955 it decided that a newspaper publisher and a journalist (Mr R. E. Fitzpatrick and Mr F. Browne of the *Bankstown Observer*) had been guilty of a serious breach of privilege for publishing articles which were intended to influence and intimidate an MP and imputing corrupt conduct by the MP for the purpose of discrediting and silencing him. The two were sent to gaol for three months. The High Court upheld the power of the House to make its findings and impose the penalty it had determined.

There have been occasional calls for the reform of the law on privilege and contempt of Parliament, and several investigations by Parliamentary committees. The last inquiry by a joint Parliamentary committee reported to the Parliament in 1984, recommending some changes in parliamentary practice. However, it rejected the idea of the Parliament exercising to the full its power under section 49 of the Constitution to produce an omnibus Act to govern the whole law of privilege and contempt. Instead it recommended some additional provisions in the form of smaller pieces of legislation, changes in Standing Orders and resolutions by the Houses, to clarify some of the contempt powers. It thought the Houses should be able to fine people who were found guilty of contempt. In 1985 the Senate Privileges Committee recommended that a newspaper organisation be put on a good behaviour bond for what it thought was a serious contempt—the publication of evidence given in secret to a Senate committee. On several occasions editors of newspapers have been required to apologise to the House or the Senate for the publication of editorials or articles which reflected on the conduct of Members or Senators.

CHAPTER 11

Law Makers

Who are the people who come to Canberra as Members of Parliament or Senators? What sort of work do they really do? What rewards do they get?

A parliamentarian's job is not everyone's idea of a great career. Politicians do not have the prestige or incomes of many doctors or barristers or other important professional people. The ordinary backbencher sitting on the Government side has, as an individual, comparatively little political power. The person sitting on the Opposition benches—whether frontbench or backbench—has no real power at all—only the possibility that at some future election he will be able to do the things he dreams and schemes and works towards achieving.

The possibility of real power and prestige (and a place in the nation's history) rests with those parliamentarians who become the leaders of their parties. Many parliamentarians begin their careers with their eyes on the top spots, wanting to be Prime Minister or a senior Minister, but most have to be content with a great deal less. That is not to say that they do not have a job to do as parliamentarians, or that they are not keen to perform that work to the best of their capabilities. Indeed, the growth since 1970 of committee work, both in parliamentary committees and parliamentary party committees, demonstrates the desire of a great many parliamentarians to contribute to the fullest to the work of the Parliament and the Government.

To become a member of the Commonwealth Parliament is to take on a full-time occupation, which for much of the year leaves no more than the odd hour or two for the parliamentarian to dabble in his former job or to try to keep up to date with developments in his former profession. (The same is not true about membership of all of the State Parliaments.) MPs and

Senators and required by their political parties to attend Parliament on a full-time basis, leave being granted only for such things as illness, or for travel abroad on parliamentary or government business. From February to June, and from August to December, the MP or Senator can expect to spend at least two weeks in every four in Canberra attending parliamentary sittings. More of his time throughout the whole of the year will be taken up with committee work. And back in his electorate he and his secretary will have to deal with thousands of enquiries each year from people he represents, who will want him to make representations for them about pensions or citizenship, to advise them about contacts with departments or Ministers, or to intervene on their behalf in some dispute with Telecom or some other government agency. The MP acts as a general ombudsman for the people who live in his electorate, trying to sort out difficulties and provide advice, often in areas which extend beyond federal government responsibilities. The amount of work the MP will have to do in his electorate, will depend on the type of electorate he represents. A wealthy Sydney or Melbourne electorate will put fewer demands on its representative than a working-class district which contains many migrants. A large electorate (thousands of square kilometres) will require its member to spend more of his time travelling than will an inner metropolitan area.

Pay and allowances

Few people doubt the need to pay parliamentarians a proper salary. There was little objection when the Australian colonies began making arrangements for paying members of their Parliaments in the 19th century, so that ordinary people could take part in the business of Parliament and Government. When the Commonwealth of Australia was formed, the Constitution made special provision for the payment of members (and this was some eleven years before the British House of Commons made permanent arrangements for the payment of its members). The Constitution gave the Parliament itself the power to decide what the salaries of its members should be, but set the salary at four hundred pounds a year until the Parliament actually used its power.

Politicians have always found it difficult to set their own salaries. It is never a good time (politically) to alter parliamentary salaries. There are no votes to be won, but lots of political cynicism to be aroused, by increasing parliamentary salaries. Most salary changes have tended to be arranged only after Government and Opposition have agreed, so that both sides would be tarred with the same brush (after all, both sides benefit from a salary increase). In 1952 Sir Robert Menzies as Prime Minister introduced a new means of altering parliamentary salaries. He appointed an independent inquiry to report on the need for salary increases, and then was able to have the Parliament adopt its recommendations. Similar inquiries were held in 1955, 1959 and 1971, and most of their recommendations were adopted in legislation passed by the Parliament. The 1971 inquiry, conducted by a federal judge, Mr Justice Kerr (later, Sir John Kerr) also recommended the creation of what in effect would be a permanent inquiry into parliamentary salaries. This would be carried out by a Remuneration Tribunal of three people, one of whom would be a judge, reporting each year to the Parliament. The recommendation was largely adopted and approved by Parliament in the Remuneration Tribunals Act. The Tribunal sets parliamentary salaries and allowances, and the salaries of other senior officials, including judges and the top public servants. The Tribunal has two separate functions in relation to parliamentarians. It merely reports to the Government on its recommendations covering the salaries which should be paid to Ministers and Judges (which means that there has to be legislation brought into Parliament to give effect to those recommendations). However, the Tribunal has been given the power to actually set the salaries and allowances to be paid to MPs and Senators and parliamentary office holders (as well as to senior public servants). It requires positive action by the Parliament to stop these increases coming into effect.

The new system was supposed to make it easier for parliamentary salaries to be increased without a political backlash, but this aim has not been entirely achieved. Although basic parliamentary salary changes are supposed to take effect automatically, Governments still find that they have to determine what their attitude will be to those increases. On several occasions Governments have found it necessary to intervene in the system. Decisions by Governments resulted in there being no salary increases during the Fraser Government's wage freeze in 1982, and increases after then were limited by the Hawke Government's prices and incomes policy in 1983–84. The consequence has been that, in the words of the 1985 Remuneration Tribunal, 'members of the Parliament. . .continue to suffer a significant disadvantage in relation to their basic salary'.

The principles which were applied by the Menzies inquiries

and the subsequent Remuneration Tribunal have generally been along the lines spelt out by the first report of the Remuneration Tribunal in 1974:

> That the Parliamentary salary should not be so low as to constitute an entry barrier to gifted and highly-qualified persons is beyond argument. The salary level at which this barrier may be created for an increasing number of well-educated and experienced persons in the professions and in technological and business pursuits is a matter of judgment. We deem it of special importance that the Parliament attracts as Members sufficient numbers of able persons to ensure in the ministries of the future the breadth of expertise and experience required to meet the demands of Government.

Mr Justice Kerr in 1971 pointed out that parliamentarians were among the high income earners in the community—though not among of the highest. He also thought that 'The salary should not be so low as to constitute an effective barrier to the able and the politically dedicated. On the other hand the salary should not be so high as to attract as candidates in most cases persons interested predominantly in the financial rewards'. He pointed out that factors other than money would influence possible political candidates. On the negative side there were the hours of work, disruption of family life, and incessant travelling. Attractions other than money included the exercise or prospect of political power, participation in the processes of Government and Opposition, the prestige of membership of the national Parliament, the opportunity for community and national service, travel, and the availability of a forum for the expression of views.

All of the inquiries rejected the idea of tying parliamentary salaries to an external indicator—either in the form of a statistical index of some kind, or the salary level of some other group in the community, such as senior public servants or academics, or some professional group. Mr Justice Kerr said there was no direct connection or comparability between the work of these other occupations (or any other occupation) and the work of a Member of Parliament. He also pointed out that MPs did not work for an employer in the accepted sense. Yet the various inquiries have also rejected the idea of what in ordinary arbitration would be a 'work value' case. Recent inquiries have accepted that MPs and Senators have a much greater work load now than used to be the case, but they have attempted to compensate for this by increasing the staffing made available to help individual MPs and Senators.

There have also been some increases in the perquisites available to parliamentarians (overseas visits, for example, and more opportunities for spouses to travel to Canberra). But by almost any measure the relative incomes of parliamentarians have fallen while their workloads (and possibly their responsibilities) have increased.

It has also been accepted that Australian parliamentarians should be paid to be full-time Members of Parliament, and that they should not have to rely on some other occupation or benefit to top up their salaries to a proper level. That principle has not been true in Britain, where many conservative MPs work as lawyers or businessmen during the day, and attend Parliament in the evening, and where many Labor MPs have their salaries or expenses supplemented by trade unions. British MPs are sometimes paid as parliamentary consultants by outside pressure groups. The reason for this is that the basic salary for a British MP is comparatively low—about two-thirds that of Australian MPs though only about half of what Australian MPs and Senators receive in pay and allowances. British Ministers are paid at about the same level as Australian Ministers.

For their full-time work, Australian MPs and Senators are well paid by general community standards, and are among the higher income earners. From 1 July 1985 the basic salary of federal parliamentarians was $42 889 a year. They also received an electorate allowance of from $15 869 to $23 010, depending on the size of the electorate they represented. Other benefits include first class air travel within Australia when on parliamentary or electorate business; a travelling allowance when staying away from home overnight ($95 in Canberra, $110 in other capital cities and $85 elsewhere); a first-class, round-the-world air fare each three years, after serving in one Parliament; a free home telephone; free postage for almost 22 000 letters a year; free long-distance phone calls and telegrams; free office accommodation in Parliament House and in an electorate office; the equivalent of three full-time electorate staff (four in very large electorates where an MP is entitled to two electorate offices); and some limited free transport to Canberra and around Australia for an MP's spouse and family. MPs and Senators who are defeated at an election or who retire are also entitled to various amounts of free domestic travel (for non-commercial purposes) for periods which depend on the length of time they were members of the Parliament—a person who served in two Parliaments would be entitled to twelve months free travel. After twenty years in Parliament, the Member is entitled to a 'Life Gold Pass' for travel for himself and his spouse throughout Australia.

Special allowances for Ministers and other office holders

Ministers and office holders such as the Speaker and party Whips receive additional salaries and allowances on top of their basic salaries and allowances as MPs or Senators. The following table lists only about a third of the office holders and the benefits they were to receive as at July 1985, but indicates the range of additional payments they receive.

OFFICE	SALARY $	EXPENSES ALLOWANCE $
Prime Minister	47 233	22 101
Deputy Prime Minister	32 195	13 034
Treasurer	25 733	11 051
Govt Leader in Senate	25 733	11 051
Other Ministers	21 361	9 067
Leader of Opposition	24 751	11 051
President	24 731	9 067
Speaker	24 731	9 067
Deputy Opposition Leader	14 148	9 067
Senate Opposition Leader	14 148	9 067
Chairman of Committees	7 520	1 869
Govt Whip, Reps	7 130	1 869
Opposition Whip, Reps	6 238	1 869
Chair, Pub. Accounts and Pub. Works committees	5 570	1 869
Chair, Senate, House standing committees	2 089	1 869

Ministers and the more senior office holders were entitled to somewhat higher travelling allowances than the allowances for MPs and Senators.

Qualifications

Almost anyone can become a Member of Parliament. To stand for Parliament, a person has to be at least eighteen years old; a British subject who has been resident in Australia for at least three years; and qualified as an elector who can vote in a House of Representatives election (this last provision excludes anyone who is of 'unsound mind' or holds a temporary entry permit or is a prohibited immigrant). A person is disqualified from election if he or she is the subject or citizen of a foreign power or owes allegiance, obedience or adherence to a foreign power; has been convicted of treason; has been convicted and is under sentence or subject to be sentenced for any offence punishable by imprisonment for a year or longer; is an undischarged bankrupt or insolvent; holds an office of profit under the Crown (though there are some exceptions to this, e.g. Ministers and retired members of the armed forces); people with various specified financial interests with the public service; and people who within the previous two years have been convicted of bribery and some other election offences.

But once all those formal requirements are satisfied, the one real test and qualification for membership of the Australian Parliament is the ability to obtain the necessary votes at an election for either the House of Representatives or the Senate. The usual prerequisite for this is to obtain endorsement from a major political party in an area in which the party can obtain majority support from the voters. The art of persuading the party to provide that endorsement, or of persuading the electorate, is part of the art of politics and an essential quality for any aspiring politician.

But parties and electorates generally require a great deal more of the people seeking their endorsement than the fact that a person wants to get into Parliament. Because the competition for parliamentary places has been increasing, parties have been able to be very choosy about the people they endorse. One result has been an increase in the status and the academic qualifications held by MPs and Senators. Once, the Labor Party was represented in Parliament mainly by trade union officials representing blue collar workers. But its representatives over the past few decades have been less obviously working class. Since the late 1960s, for example, the number of doctors and dentists among its parliamentarians has outnumbered those in Liberal Party ranks. The Liberal Party still sends twice as many lawyers to Parliament as Labor, and more company directors and managers, and former members of the armed services, but Labor has more former university lecturers, retailers and public servants and diplomats. Less than half the members of the National Party are farmers or graziers, the Liberal Party having almost as many people in this category as the National Party and the Labor Party includes several in its ranks. Lawyers are the largest individual group in the Liberal Party, while teachers and lecturers form the largest group in the Labor Party. In the 1983 Parliament, two-thirds of the MPs and Senators had at least two higher academic qualifications, and the qualifications held ranged from Ph.D.s to Diplomas.

The Parliament was a very different place in 1901 when it was first elected, and in its early years. The Labor Party at that stage had little support outside the trade unions (which were based on blue collar and rural workers). The first Labor Government had to call on a person from another party to be its Attorney-General, because it did not then have a lawyer among its parliamentary ranks.

Looking back only to the early 1960s it is possible to see quite substantial changes in the composition of the Parliament. At the end of 1962 the Country Party was absolutely dominated by primary producers—seventeen of its twenty-three parliamentarians being in that category. Twenty-one years later eight of the National Party's parliamentarians were primary producers. The largest group in the Liberal Party were also primary producers—sixteen out of sixty-nine (in 1983, six out of fifty-six). The other major occupational groups in the Liberal Party were lawyers (thirteen, compared with eighteen in 1983), and company directors or business executives (ten, compared with seven in 1983). Labor ranks in 1962 were dominated by union officials (sixteen out of ninety in the Caucus) and former public servants, thirteen. In 1983 there were eleven former union officials out of 105 members of Caucus and nine former public servants. The other groups now heavily represented were teachers (eleven, compared with five, twenty-one years earlier) and university lecturers (ten, compared with three in the earlier Parliament).

Comparison of the educational qualifications of the MPs and Senators from the two Parliaments shows that the 1983 Parliament had about twice as many members with degrees and diplomas as the 1962 Parliament. In the earlier Parliament twenty-eight MPs and Senators had B.A.s or M.A.s—fifty-five of the 1983 parliamentarians had those degrees. There were seventeen members of the 1962 Parliament with law degrees, and this increased to thirty-two in the later Parliament. There were two members of the 1962 Parliament with medical degrees and two with Doctorates of Philosophy, but six medical doctors and six Ph.D.s in 1983. (Only five men were members of both Parliaments.)

The 1983 Parliament was middle-aged, rather than elderly (as is sometimes the image of Parliament). There were two MPs under thirty years old, but only one over sixty-five. Almost a quarter were between forty-five and forty-nine, but a third of the Parliament were under forty-five. Senators on average were slightly older than MPs. About half the Senators were fifty or over, while about a third of MPs were in that age group.

Partly because there was a change of Government in 1983,

resulting from a fairly large number of electoral defeats for sitting MPs in that election, the 1983 Parliament contained a very large number of new MPs. By the end of 1983, a quarter of the MPs had been in Parliament for less than a year. But a fifth of them had been there for only one Parliament (three years) and another sixth for an additional Parliament. This meant that well over half the Members of the House of Representatives had been in Parliament for less than seven years.

Another difference between present Parliaments and older ones is the presence of women in both the House of Representatives and the Senate. The first women were not elected to the Parliament until 1943, when the widow of a former non-Labor Prime Minister was elected to the House of Representatives, and a Labor Senator was elected to the Senate. By 1983 a total of twenty-nine women had been elected to the Commonwealth Parliament, twenty of them in the Senate. In 1983 of the sixty-four Senators thirteen were women. There were then six women members of the House of Representatives, including the Chairman of Committees. Since 1975 both Liberal and Labor Cabinets have included one woman Cabinet Minister.

Very few people would plan their working lives to eventually make a career out of being a member of Parliament, though for some, membership of Parliament is the result of a great deal of work and planning. But many parliamentarians are attracted to a life of politics by accident. They become politically activated by some event—such as depression or war or a demonstration or some economic calamity—and their desire to 'do something' leads them towards Parliament. Occasionally MPs find themselves in Parliament without having thought about the desirability of such a move—they have accepted pre-selection for a seat held by the other side, and there has been an unexpectedly large swing which has catapulted them into Parliament. Occasionally someone is approached by a party to stand even though he has not been active politically—the party concerned may not have had a candidate it considered suitable, or it may have thought that the particular qualities of the person were such that he would attract votes the party would not otherwise obtain. But once in Parliament, there are few MPs or Senators who willingly resign to return to their previous careers.

Ethics and honesty

Australian parliamentarians may work hard and be well paid for their labours, but they do not enjoy great public esteem. Public opinion polls show that federal politicians rank quite low on a scale of occupations for 'honesty and ethical standards'. While doctors, dentists and bank managers rate over 60 per cent, federal politicians were down to 13 per cent in the 1975 poll. More surprisingly, the rating of politicians has slumped over the past decade. In 1976 their rating was 19 per cent. No other occupational group, apart from state parliamentarians, had undergone such a substantial fall in public perceptions.

Over the past decade and a half, federal politicians have been moving towards some form of scheme in which they would have to disclose pecuniary and other interests which might affect the way they carried out their duties. Ministers now have to make declarations to the Prime Minister of their financial interests and the House of Representatives has decided that its members should make similar declarations. However, the disclosure of such interests by backbench and Opposition MPs has been opposed by the Liberal and National parties. At the time of writing the House of Representatives was still considering the form in which such declarations should be made, while the Senate had made no move towards embracing any disclosure system at all. The schemes which have been considered for disclosure all take as their starting point the fact that there have been no significant charges of financial or any other kinds of irregularities directed against federal Ministers or MPs in recent years, and that what is sought to be avoided is any possible suggestion that there could be improprieties in the conduct of the federal Parliament.

CHAPTER 12

Making Parliament Work

More than a thousand people work behind the scene to ensure that Parliament, and parliamentarians, function properly. Some are members of the staff of the five Parliamentary Departments (established quite separately and distinctly from the Public Service). Others work directly as secretaries and researchers for politicians, paid for by the Government, but answerable only to their particular MP or Senator. An entirely separate group of people who work in the parliamentary Press Gallery are employed by newspapers, and radio and television stations throughout Australia. They are responsible (but only to their employers) for reporting to the public just what the Parliament and its members do.

Parliamentary Departments

There are five separate Parliamentary Departments. The Departments of the House of Representatives and the Senate, The Parliamentary Library, the Parliamentary Reporting Services, and the Joint House Department. The Department of the House of Representatives looks after everything which happens in the House, and after many of the facilities of its Members. Inside the chamber the most prominent are the Clerk and his Deputy, sitting at the top of the centre table, below the Speaker's Chair. The Clerk is on hand to give the Speaker or Chairman of Committees advice about the conduct of procedure and the interpretation of Standing Orders. He also controls the recording of everything which happens in the House—what matters are discussed and decided. He notes any documents or petitions which are presented to the House, and ensures that all the documentation associated with the passage of Bills through the House, and to and from the Senate and the Governor-General, is correct. The Clerk is also the head of the staff of the Department of the House of Representatives— the equivalent of the permanent head of a Public Service department. The person he is responsible to for the running of his department is not a Minister (as would be the case with a Public Service department) but the Speaker of the House of Representatives.

The Department of the House of Representatives was staffed by about 180 people at the beginning of 1985. The largest group were in the Committee Office, and provided secretariats for all the House Committees, and some joint committees. The Office of the Serjeant-at-Arms looked after Members' accommodation, facilities and services, ceremonial and security. Other sections provided the backing for the work of the Clerk in the Chamber, and helped control the vast flood of paper which engulfs Members. The House had its own printing and photocopying sections, which in recent years were producing over three million pages a year.

The Department of the Senate is organised in a very similar way to the House, with about the same total staff. There is a slightly greater concentration in the Senate's operation on providing support for committees. This reflects the greater emphasis on committee work undertaken by the Senate. Both the House and the Senate Departments also have sections responsible for parliamentary relations. This is a reference to relations with other Parliaments, mainly overseas. They look after visits by other parliamentarians to Australia, and by Australian MPs and Senators to other countries. The Senate looks after relations with the Commonwealth Parliamentary Association, which has as its Members all the Parliaments of Australia and the (British) Commonwealth. The House of Representatives staff are responsible for Australia's relations with the Inter-Parliamentary Union, the major international association of Members of Parliament.

The Parliamentary Library plays a vital part in the provision of information services to MPs and Senators. The Parliament began the creation of its own library shortly after the Parliament itself came into being in 1901. When the Parliament moved to Canberra in 1927, its library was the only library in the new national capital, so it had to provide a domestic service, as well as the beginnings of a national library, and a library for the Canberra University College, in addition to its parliamentary function. In the 1960s the Parliament was able to shed the last of these additional functions and concentrate on servicing the Members of Parliament and others associated with the Parliament. It did in fact greatly expand these services by creating a legislative reference service, and greatly expanding its general reference and information services.

The bulk of the library is situated between the two parliamentary chambers on the ground and lower ground floors of the main parliamentary building. The main entrance from King's Hall leads into a foyer in which all of the Australian daily newspapers are kept on file. In the main library area are thousands of reference books, journals, weekly magazines, and books covering a wide range of subjects. A current information service, which provides clippings of all the major newspapers on current affairs topics, is serviced mainly from the lower ground floor. This service also records and transcribes all the ABC radio and television news and current affairs programs which are transmitted in Canberra. The current information service receives over 12 000 requests a year for access to files or to transcripts.

The Legislative Research Service provides background papers and research information covering the whole field of government. It has sections covering defence, economics and commerce, education and welfare, foreign affairs, law and government, science technology and environment, and statistics. It receives over 5000 requests a year from MPs and Senators, and while half of them require less than an hour's work to answer, many hundreds of the requests take more than a day's work. The answers, which may be in the form of notes which can be used for a speech, or a series of tables, or an interpretation of statistics, are made available only to the MP or Senator who requested them, but can then be used without restriction in debate, or political party activity, in committee work, or the electorate, or published through the media. The basic data in an answer will be provided to any parliamentarian who asks for it. As well as answering requests, the service publishes general papers which are available to all Members. These include briefs on current affairs topics, a monthly list of economic and social indicators, discussion papers and background papers. Recent papers include a 26-page discussion paper on Power Generation Options in Tasmania: Thermal vs Interconnection Options, and a current affairs brief entitled 'A short guide to nuclear weapons and warfare terminology'. Regular bulletins are produced on financial indicators, the budget and state elections.

The Legislative Reference Service answers requests for factual information, again on the whole range of government activity, both domestic and foreign. Its sources are reference books and written materials, and a large range of on-line (i.e. direct access) computer data bases, some of them overseas. It has almost immediate access to the information resources of the National Library, and rapid access to most other libraries throughout Australia.

Services of a different kind are provided by the Joint House Department, which looks after the general fabric of the Parliament House building, and the grounds around it, which include squash courts, bowling greens, a cricket pitch, two volley-ball courts and five tennis courts. It also provides more basic services: food and drink and general housekeeping services. And it is responsible for the Parliament House guides, bookshop and displays, for ceremonial and hospitality outside the two chambers, and for security services around Parliament.

Security has been of increasing importance since the late 1970s. It was not until the bomb attack on the Sydney Hilton Hotel, during the holding of the Commonwealth Heads of Government Regional meeting when several City Council employees were killed in a bomb outrage, that the Parliament introduced security screening of visitors, to ensure that no weapons were brought into Parliament House by any of the half-million or so visitors who go through the Parliament each year. There have been occasional incidents when protesters have waved banners inside the Parliamentary Chambers and even thrown flour bombs, but no attacks have been made on parliamentarians. The security net is loose enough to allow the normal functioning of the Parliament at most times—all staff and people who need regular access to the building are issued with photographic passes, while the security staff are trained to recognize the 200 plus Members and Senators (who do not wear badges). But for VIP visits, even pass holders have to go through bomb and weapon detection units, and major sweeps are made through the building to ensure that it is clear of offensive weapons.

The Department of the Parliamentary Reporting Staff is responsible for producing *Hansard*, the official record of the debates of the House and the Senate and of their committees. The reporting staff also produces records of debates for the Premiers Conference and other ministerial meetings, and national and parliamentary conferences, particularly those held in the parliament building. However, not all the official records of the Parliament are produced by *Hansard*. The House of Representatives produces its own official record of *Votes and Proceedings*, which records all of the business proceedings in the House such as its decisions and votes, and the presentation of various petitions and papers. But it does not record speeches. The Senate produces a *Journal* which has a similar function. And both Houses are responsible for the production of their own *Notice Papers*.

Hansard is produced in several stages. Reporters (there are about thirty altogether) sit in the two Chambers to take shorthand notes (either manually or by machine). Each reporter does a five-minute 'take' of the proceedings, and then immediately returns to the *Hansard* office to have this typed. This first version is checked by a *Hansard* supervisor (who normally will have done a one-hour stint in the Chamber) and a copy (a 'pink' or a 'green') given to the Senator or Member who made the speech, or asked the question, which was covered by the reporter. Minor corrections can be made at this stage, to ensure that the rules of grammar are properly observed and that the report accurately reflects what was said. (MPs are not allowed to change the sense of what they said, or to correct factual errors they made when speaking. To do that, they should make a correction in Parliament itself.) The *Hansard* does not pretend to be a complete verbatim account of everything that was said in the Parliament. Interjections, for example, are only recorded if they are responded to by the MP or Senator who is speaking, or if they provoke some reaction from the Presiding Officer. Overnight, the whole of the proceedings for the day are collated and indexed, and what is referred to as a daily proof *Hansard* for each House is printed by the Government Printer. Corrections can still be made by Members to this version. Later, the corrected proofs are printed in weekly volumes (in green or red covers—the proof issue was simply a white-paper-covered volume). At the end of the year bound volumes of *Hansard* are produced which contain a very detailed index.

The *Hansard* reporter is expected to be able to write shorthand at at least 150 words a minute—fast enough to cover fairly quick speakers. But all the proceedings of the Houses are recorded, so that a reporter can check his notes against a tape. Most committee reports are recorded only through the transcription of tape recordings of the committee's proceedings. Increasingly, *Hansard* is using word processors rather than typewriters to produce its reports.

Parliamentarians' staff

Each MP and Senator is entitled to have a personal staff of three full-time employees paid for by the Government. Two at least must be located back in the offices provided for the politicians in their home electorates and they are generally the first point of contact for members of the public seeking the help of their parliamentary representative. The other staff member may be based either in the electorate or in Canberra, sharing the MP's parliamentary office. The MP or Senator can divide his staff entitlement (worth about $65 000 at the beginning of 1985) among a greater number of part-time workers if he wishes. The MP can also provide up to fifteen interstate trips a year for his staff to bring a staff member to Canberra or transfer him to the electorate office temporarily, or to accompany the MP on parliamentary business elsewhere. Most MPs use their staff entitlements to ensure that they have one or two secretary/stenographers, and a research assistant who also helps with writing speeches or media material. A lack of space in offices in the old Parliament House prevents parliamentarians making full use of their staff during parliamentary sittings.

Ministers have additional staff to help them with their official duties. Most have three or four senior advisers, sometimes including a press secretary, and three or four typists/stenographers.

Public Servants

A great many public servants have passes to enter Parliament House but most of them are concerned with the work of the Government rather than the Parliament. Senior Departmental officials are regular callers on Ministers, and members of the Department of Prime Minister and Cabinet have to service the regular meetings of the Cabinet and its committees.

Two public servants have a very direct influence on the Parliament, however. These are the Parliamentary Liaison Officers, who work in the offices of the Leader of the House (of Representatives) and the Manager of Government Business (in the Senate). Their task is to help the two Houses to function in as smooth a way as possible, and they often act as intermediaries between Government and Opposition, trying to ensure that matters come on for debate at agreed times and for agreed periods. However, their posts are filled by public servants rather than by parliamentary officers because they also take part in advising relevant Cabinet committees about the progress of legislation before it reaches the Parliament, as well as after its introduction.

Many other public servants are called to the Parliament to provide assistance to parliamentary and party committees. Strict guidelines have been developed in the past ten years for public servants giving evidence to party and parliamentary committees because of the much greater use those committees have been making of public servants. While the public servants are made available quite freely for briefings on legislation or Government decisions, they are required not to express opinions on matters of policy or party-political issues. The guidelines require the public servants not to advocate, defend or canvass the merits of Government policies, including the policies of present and past Governments, federal and state; and not to identify the particular considerations which led the Government to adopt a policy unless those considerations have already been made public by a Minister. However, they may describe policies and administrative arrangements involved in implementing them; and they may set out policy options and list advantages and disadvantages of various policy options provided they do not do so in a politically partisan way, and provided the Government wants such options canvassed.

The group of public servants whose work is most intimately bound up with that of the Parliament is the staff of the Parliamentary Counsel. They are responsible for the drafting of all the Bills which are presented to the Parliament, and for all the amendments which the Government may propose. Because they rarely have any free time available for the drafting of Private Members' Bills or Opposition and minor party amendments, the Senate since 1982 has made available a small amount for the hiring of consultants to help private Members in the highly technical process of drafting legislation or amendments.

The Press Gallery

Most people know what is happening in Parliament House only through the reports carried in the Australian media—in the press, on radio and on television—and not through the official *Hansard* reports. The picture they get is certainly not a full one, and it is not always accurate. And primarily, it is concerned with the activities of Government and the confrontations and personalities of politics, not with the work of Parliament.

The relationship between parliamentarians and the media is an odd one. The 150 or so members of the Press Gallery are the only non-Government or non-Parliament employees in the building. They owe their allegiance to their various editors and employers, not to the Parliament. They report comparatively little of what is actually said in the Parliament, but what they do report is vitally important for the public's understanding of what happens there. This is because the official record, *Hansard*, and the official broadcasts of parliamentary proceedings, through the ABC, reach comparatively few people. Voters generally know only what they read in the papers, hear on radio, or see on television, of the goings-on in Parliament House. Those goings-on include the work of Government as well as of the Parliament, and the general political toings and froings of the national political parties—irrespective of whether the events being described actually happen in Parliament, or even Canberra. The Press Gallery is the base for national political reporters and commentators. Reporting precisely what the Parliament does is an extremely small proportion of their work.

And yet the Parliament provides them with free quarters immediately next to the parliamentary chambers and every possible access to the Parliament. Separate galleries are set aside in both the House of Representatives (two galleries) and the Senate (one) for the media's representatives, but those in the House are fully occupied only during Question Time and times of high political drama while the Senate Press Gallery attracts a full house only during ceremonial occasions, such as the official opening of the Parliament. Most of the reporting of what happens in the parliamentary chambers is performed by a press agency, Australian Associated Press, which supplies its services to most media organisations throughout Australia. Among major media organisations, only the ABC attempts to provide an independent report of what happens in the Parliament, though most of the capital city morning papers will provide their own reports of the major issues which arise at Question Time, and of important Government announcements and political clashes which occur in the Parliament.

At the geographic centre of the media accommodation in Parliament are two sets of boxes into which MPs and Senators, Ministers and their departments, lobbyists and pressure groups, and anyone else who knows of their existence and wants to try to get something reported by the media, put their press releases and reports. Journalists read through or glance at all the material deposited in their boxes, to see whether any of it would be 'newsworthy' in accordance with the particular needs of their own newspaper, magazine, radio or television station. Only a small proportion of it is transmitted to the journalist's head office, and not all of what is sent is then printed or broadcast.

Journalists in the Press Gallery are free to wander through most of the corridors of the Parliament. They are barred from just a few areas—for example, the area immediately outside the Cabinet room, part of the library, some of the Members' dining and refreshments rooms, and the party meeting rooms. Their freedom makes it easier for them to make direct personal contact with the politicians, officials and staff on whom they rely for much of the material which they write. Journalists and politicians depend greatly on each other. Journalists look to politicians to provide them with information and advice, with the 'leaks' which are essential if a journalist is to build his reputation and which a news organisation needs to promote itself. Politicians need to cultivate individual journalists to ensure that their names become well known and their ideas and personal qualities favourably regarded. Politicians and journalists exchange views of politics and policies and personalities.

The main concern of the Press Gallery is with breaking 'news' stories—stories which will be published by their news organisation and which their readers or listeners or viewers will find interesting. Over the years the appreciation by editors and journalists of what their public wants from them has changed. Before radio and television, newspapers reported the debates in the Parliament at some length, explaining the content of the fewer, less complex pieces of legislation the Parliament considered. They also told their readers about the personalities of their politicians, party splits, policy divisions, crises and rows. Over the years the emphasis has increased on reporting that last group of political developments, at the expense of the first. The public can have little appreciation that anything other than political skulduggery occurs.

In recent years all the television networks have established studios inside Parliament House allowing them direct contact with their Sydney and Melbourne headquarters and instant access to the air waves. One effect has been to change the way in which Ministers and politicians use the Parliament. Ministerial statements in the Parliament are timed to allow the Minister to hold a press conference elsewhere in Parliament House which can be recorded by radio and television for almost immediate use in news bulletins throughout the country. The Press conference has become a far better medium for publicity than the parliamentary debate. Parliament House is the centre for the reporting of national politics, but the focus of that reporting is not the Parliament itself.

CHAPTER 13

Elections and Electoral Systems

Australia has a unique electoral system, which combines a series of unusual features. Compulsory voting and preferential voting apply to both House of Representatives and Senate elections (and almost all State elections) but are comparatively rare overseas. In the House of Representatives each electorate elects only a single member; in the Senate each State elects twelve Senators (but normally only six at each election) while each of the two Territories each elects two Senators. The method of counting votes is different for the two Houses, the Senate adopting an unusual method of proportional representation.

Each of these features affects the result in any election, and has helped to determine the type of party system which has developed in Australia. None of the features developed automatically or inevitably; most were chosen because the party in control of the Parliament at the time a change was implemented thought it would benefit from that particular change. But not every alteration to the system produced the result which was expected from it.

And the system continues to change, with effects which are still not completely predictable. In 1984 the largest number of alterations to the system for decades came into effect, increasing the size of the Parliament by one-fifth, and introducing on to ballot papers, for the first time in federal elections, the names of the political parties which various candidates represented. A change in the method of electing the Senate succeeded in reducing what had been a chronically high informal vote for the Senate—but coincided with an unexpectedly large informal vote for the House of Representatives (though whether voters deliberately intended to bring about this result was not entirely clear).

The major features of the electoral system (in 1985) for federal elections were:

Secret ballot

It would be surprising, these days, to think of voting other than secretly; but secrecy was a feature of Australian electoral systems long before it became accepted in most other democratic countries—so much so that in some parts of the United States the notion of a secret ballot, and of the confidentiality of votes, is still referred to as the 'Australian ballot'. In fact, the Australian colonies began to introduce secret ballots in 1856, the last one doing so in 1877. This was twenty years and more before secret ballots were introduced by most other western countries.

Compulsory voting

Australia is one of the few democratic countries which compels its citizens to register as voters, and then tries to force them to exercise their 'right' to vote. Most countries make voting something of a privilege which is extended to its citizens. As a consequence, the result of an election may depend on the number of people who take the trouble to go and register a vote on election day, and that in turn can be affected by the weather, or the general interest in the election, or the likelihood of a particular result. In many communist countries voting is not compulsory, in theory, but 99 per cent voting is expected, and apparently occurs. In Britain and the United States, where voting is voluntary, the number of people actually voting may be as low as 50 per cent, or as high as 80 per cent. The last 'free' vote for the House of Representatives (in 1922) resulted in only 58 per cent of those eligible actually voting.

Australia adopted compulsory registration for most voters (that is, making all eligible voters apply to put their names on the voting roll as soon as they become eligible) as long ago as 1911 (though it did not become compulsory for Aborigines to register until 1984; indeed most Aborigines were unable to vote until 1977). Compulsion to vote (for all those who had their names on an electoral roll) was first introduced in Queensland in 1915 and in Commonwealth referendums the following year. Compulsion to vote at elections was introduced by the Commonwealth Parliament in 1924, and over the next fifteen years by all the States.

But 'compulsion' is a relative term. Until 1983 the penalty for failing to register as a voter was not less than $1, nor more than $4. For failing to vote the penalty was from $2 to $10. In 1983 the (maximum) penalty for each offence was increased to $50. And while it is compulsory to enrol and then to vote, the fact that a vote is secret means that it cannot be made illegal to vote informally—that is, so that the vote simply does not count in determining who wins the election. To a minor extent, informal votes probably represent the votes of some of the people who would stay away from polling booths on election day if they had the choice.

Preferential voting

The basic idea behind preferential voting is that no one should be elected to represent a group of people unless he or she represents the majority of the people in the electorate. When more than two people stand for an election it is always possible that the person with the most votes, will not have a majority (i.e., more than half the total number of votes). In some countries the problem is over-come by having a second election, between the top two candidates. In Australia the same kind of elimination contest is carried out by the voter when he marks his voting card. He tells the electoral office his order of preference of the candidates, from top to bottom. This is done by putting a number against the name of every person listed on the ballot paper—if there are five candi-dates, the voter has to decide which of them is to get his 1 vote, then which should get 2, then 3, 4 and finally 5.

When the votes are counted, if one candidate gets more than half the 1 votes, he is declared elected. But if no one gets a majority, the candidate with the smallest number of 1s is elimi-nated, and his votes are given to those candidates who were marked as 2 on the eliminated candidate's ballot papers. If there is still no one with a majority, the candidate with the next lowest number of 1s is eliminated, and his 2 preferences distributed to the other candidates. The process continues until one candidate does have more than half the votes.

The preferential voting system is more complicated than the 'first past the post' system—where voters only have to put a mark against the name of one candidate, and the person with the highest number of votes wins, whether or not he has more than half the votes. This simplest of voting methods was used in House of Rep-resentatives voting until 1918. The preferential voting method does cause a certain number of 'informal' or invalid votes, resulting from people not putting a number in every square, or putting the same number more than once (a mistake which can easily be made if there are a large number of candidates, and the voter wants to skip all over the ballot paper to try to write down his particular order of preference among the candidates).

Each electorate, one MP

The Constitution makes it clear that the number of MPs in the House of Representatives should mirror (approximately) the dif-ferent populations of the different States, and that the members of the House of Representatives should be directly chosen by the people (and not, for example, by State Parliaments). The Com-monwealth Electoral Act takes this one step further and divides Australia into the same number of electoral divisions (or elector-ates) as there are Members of the House of Representatives. This means that each electorate is represented in the House of Rep-resentatives by just one MP.

Electorates based on equal number of voters

The Constitution gives each of the present States a minimum of five Members of the House of Representatives, but for the rest, the number of MPs per State depends on State populations. In recent years the fact that Victoria and New South Wales have grown at a slower rate than Queensland and Western Australia resulted in the latter two States increasing their representation in the House of Representatives at the expense of the larger States. But overall, the number of MPs from a State reflects the different populations of the States.

However, the Constitution does not spell out just how States are to be divided up into the various electorates. This is done in the Electoral Act, which sets up machinery to say who should determine electoral boundaries, when they should be changed, and what matters have to be taken into account in deciding where boundaries should go.

Electoral boundaries are drawn by independent Commissioners, and since the 1983 changes to the Electoral Act the final determinations of the Commissioners are not liable to be overturned by the Parliament. The main aim of the Commissioners in deciding just where the boundaries of each electorate will be is to try to ensure that all the electorates in a State will, in a further three and a half years time, have as nearly as practicable the same number of electors. The idea of looking forward three and a half years is to produce a system which only needs to be changed every seven years. To obtain equality at that future point, the Commissioners are able to draw boundaries in which some electorates will vary up to 10 per cent from the average number of electors per electorate for the State. In the past the Electoral Act has sometimes allowed variations of 20 per cent from the average size of electorates, and encouraged Commissioners to take into account the large size of some electorates—the idea being that the larger country electorates could have smaller voting populations. However, this idea has now been eliminated from the Act, though Commissioners can take account of such things as the physical features and area of an electoral division, means of communication within it, and community of interests. But the overriding concern now is equality of electors—a means of achieving the idea of one vote-one value (all electors having the same voting power).

Redistributions

The system provides for redistributions whenever there is a

change in the number of representatives to be elected from a State (which means there would have to be a change in the number of electorates); whenever more than a third of the electorates in a State differ from the average enrolment in the State by more or less than 10 per cent; and seven years after the last redistribution. The Commissioners call for submissions from the public, including political parties, and publish their initial recommendations of new boundaries. After considering any objections to these, the Commissioners can then formally declare the new electoral boundaries.

The initial redistribution is carried out by a committee which consists of the Commonwealth Electoral Commissioner, the Australian electoral officer for the state, the Surveyor-General for the State and the Auditor-General for the State. To this group is added the full Commonwealth Electoral Commission when any objections are to be determined. The Commission, which governs the whole conduct of the Commonwealth electoral system, consists of two part-time members—the Chairman, who must be a judge, and a permanent head of a public service department—together with the Electoral Commissioner, who is the chief executive officer of the Commission.

Ballot paper: party names

The 1983 changes to the Electoral Act gave the Electoral Office permission for the first time to list the names of political parties against the names of election candidates. Previously, voters had to rely on advertising, or their own personal interest, or on election material handed out in front of the polling booths to discover which parties the various candidates were standing for. Governments were reluctant to agree to the names of political parties appearing on ballot papers. However, the 1983 amendments brought in an entirely new system of regulating party names in order to ensure that voters would not be confused by new or break-away parties trying to capitalise on the name of a well-established political party. The law even prevents anyone from starting a party called the 'Independent' party because the word 'Independent' is still used to describe people who do not belong to any party at all. But the new system does not prevent new political parties being started, because it allows the registration of any party which has 500 members.

Ballot paper: positions

Traditionally, the alphabet has decided order in which people's names should be listed in all kinds of activities. While this is very useful in a publication like the telephone book, where you want to locate a particular person's name, it is not so successful as a means of listing candidates standing for an election, because it tends to be unfair to those whose names begin with letters which are not high in the alphabet. It has been found that some people simply vote down the ballot paper, when faced with a list of people whom they don't know, or in a situation in which they have no interest in the eventual result (two circumstances which do result sometimes from the compulsory voting system). This presumably unthinking straight down the paper vote became known as the 'donkey vote'.

The alphabetical list system was abandoned in Senate elections in 1940, after the Labor Party managed to produce a Senate team from New South Wales all of whom had surnames beginning with 'A'. Other parties also took note of the system and used it to their advantage (which could have been worth 1 or 2 per cent in some electorates). The result was a bias, compared with the community generally, of people in Parliament with surnames beginning with letters in the top third of the alphabet.

The Senate voting paper was changed to allow for a ballot for positions—and for placing the various party groups across the ballot paper, instead of down it. But the voting paper for the House of Representatives did not adopt the idea of a ballot for places on the ballot paper until the 1983 amendments to the Act. Top position is still thought to be an advantage, though perhaps to a lesser extent now that party names are on the ballot paper, but now the random effect of a lottery draw for positions means that, over a period of time, no particular party should win an advantage over its opponents.

Senate voting system

The problem with the Senate was that a group of people had to be elected at the same time to represent the same area. At first each State was represented by six Senators. At each normal election, three Senators would be elected for each State, but at any double dissolution, all six would have to be elected. Later the number of Senators to be elected at a normal election increased to five per State, and in 1983 to six. Ordinary first-past-the-post voting, and then preferential voting, tended to give the party which was the most popular at the time of the election more than its expected share of the number of Senators—it was not unusual for one party to win all three Senate vacancies from a State. To overcome this apparent unfairness, the system was changed in 1948 to bring in proportional representation. This system is designed to allow different parties and groups to be represented in Parliament in proportion to their voting strength. The change was accompanied by use of the preferential system. This copied to a large degree the system in use in Tasmanian State elections. Because there are comparatively few people to be elected from each State at each election, however, the system still does not favour very small parties. With six Senators to be elected from each State, a party now needs one-seventh of the total vote in the State to get a Senator elected. But with the help of preferences from parties with even smaller support, and preferences of votes left over from parties who have elected candidates, it is sometimes possible to elect a person who gets about two-thirds of the votes he would need to win in his own right. Normally, though, a candidate will need to get at least one-tenth of the vote from his state to have a reasonable chance of being elected to the Senate in an ordinary Senate election when there are six Senators to be elected.

Senate ballot paper: groups

The proportional and preferential systems used in the Senate make it desirable for parties to stand groups of candidates— generally including one more person than they have a real chance of getting elected. Parties are required to stand at least two candidates in order to get themselves listed separately on the ballot paper, rather than being pushed in with all the independent candidates in a collection of 'ungrouped' people at the end of the ballot paper. Positions on the ballot paper for each group are balloted for separately in each State.

Senate ballot paper: list voting

The 1983 amendments to the Electoral Act introduced a major change to the form and shape of the Senate ballot paper, giving voters a very easy way of indicating a preference for the party of their choice. Previously the only way of voting in Senate elections was to express a preference for every candidate—and this could be a long and tedious process when sixty or seventy people were standing for the Senate in a State. There had to be a number written by the voter in every square, and it would be easy to make a mistake and vote informally, or not be sure that a correct vote for the chosen party had been properly written out. In the 1977 elections, for example, the informal vote in the Senate election was 9 per cent, compared with about 2.5 per cent for the House of Representatives election held at the same time. A little more than half the spoilt Senate votes contained an incorrect sequence of numbers. More than a quarter of the votes were informal because some squares had not been numbered at all. One solution provided by the 1983 changes was to introduce party names on to the ballot paper (so that people would be able to identify more clearly who they wished to vote for, and to give voters an alternative to numbering every square). A new section was also added at the top of the ballot paper. This simply listed the various party groups by their names, and did not include the names of any candidates. Voters could simply mark one square, giving their vote to that party (preferences would be carried out according to the official party ticket). But voters who wanted to list candidates in their own order of preference could still do so by ignoring the top section of the ballot paper, and marking the lower section as they had previously. In fact marking the lower part was the only way in which voters would be able to vote for anyone in the 'ungrouped' category because they were not listed on the new part of the ballot.

Registration of political parties

The introduction of public funding for political parties taking part in elections (discussed in the next chapter) and the use of party names on ballot papers, made it necessary to regulate the way in which party names were used. The Parliament decided to introduce a system of registration of parties, which would be supervised by the new independent Australian Electoral Commission. Registration is available to any party which has a member in any federal, state or territory Parliament, or any other party which has at least 500 members. The rules concerning party names are designed mainly to prevent voters being misled by any new groups using names closely resembling existing political parties. The Commission is forbidden to register a party which has a name or an abbreviation the same as, or nearly the same as an unrelated party. It also cannot register any party name which contains the word independent. This prevents anyone calling themselves the Independent Party, or the Independent Liberal or Independent Labor Party. Also banned are any names which are obscene, or any which contain more than six words.

Results of the system

1. *The party system.* One of the effects of the use of preferential voting has been to allow the continuation of what is a three, or two and a half, party system in the House of Representatives. Effectively, the Government is controlled either by a coalition of the Liberal and National parties, or by the Labor Party. The preferential system has allowed the Liberal and National parties to keep their separate identities, and to oppose each other in some electorates, while maintaining their joint antagonism towards the Labor Party. A first-past-the-post voting system would make it almost impossible for the Liberal and National parties to contest an electorate against one another because the Labor Party would normally obtain the largest vote. But because the Liberals and Nationals can exchange preferences, they are able to count (in effect) their combined total against the votes obtained by Labor. The preferential system also preserved the Democratic Labor Party for a long time despite its inability to win seats in the House of Representatives. Its supporters knew they could not elect their own candidates, but by using their preferences they were able to help determine which party would be elected (in the case of the DLP, the aim was to prevent Labor ever being elected). Similarly, the preferential system preserves other smaller parties which see their role not as electing their own candidate, but as allowing them to bargain with the larger parties for preferences in exchange for particular favours—normally in the form of policies which the smaller party wants the larger party to adopt (for example, aid to state schools, or nuclear disarmament).

2. *Minor Senate parties and groups.* The combination of the preferential voting system plus proportional representation in the Senate has helped change the nature of party representation in that Chamber too. Parties, groups and individuals which cannot hope to muster 50 per cent of the vote in House of Representatives electorates find it much easier to win 10 or 12 per cent of the vote across a state.

The success of particular smaller parties and groups is affected by the number of Senators to be elected from a State at any election. The increase from five to six in the number normally elected at a Senate election is likely to make it slightly more difficult for the smaller parties, because it will be easier for the two larger party groups to elect three Senators each (for which they need only 43 per cent of the vote).

3. *Public perceptions*. Many voters regularly vote differently in the Senate from the way they do in the House. There is a greater variety of candidates and issues in the Senate. Candidates or parties can run single-issue campaigns there in a way which is not possible in the House of Representatives, where the fate of the Government is at stake. The Senate's role is seen differently, sometimes to act as a brake on the Government, sometimes to allow the advance of a particular idea. For example, the Australian Democrats have based their campaign on the notion that they will keep the Government (of whatever party) honest. The Nuclear Disarmament Party had a Senator elected on that one issue of nuclear disarmament. In the 1960s a Western Australian was elected to the Senate on the single issue of abolishing death duties. Tasmania has had a history of electing independents who have broken from the Labor Party. The electoral system in fact encourages people to use their votes in different ways for the two Houses.

4. *By-elections*. The Constitution makes different arrangements for filling vacancies which occur in the two Houses. By-elections for the House of Representatives take the same form as ordinary House elections, except that there is an election in just the one electorate where the vacancy has occurred (say, through the death or resignation of the previous Member). In the Senate the vacancy is filled by the Governor or Parliament of the State, and since the Constitution was changed in 1977, the new Senator has to be a member of the same party or group that the previous Senator belonged to.

5. *Unpredictability*. Not all the changes which have been made in the electoral system have affected the outcome of elections in quite the way their designers intended. The Labor Party, for example, introduced proportional representation in Senate elections, but that helped to perpetuate the Democratic Labor Party which came into existence just a few years later, and whose principal aim was to try to keep the Labor Party from winning government. The Labor Party's main complaints about the House of Representatives system was that the ALP needed more than 51 per cent and sometimes over 52 per cent of the national vote to win Government. Many of its 1983 changes to the system of redistributing electoral boundaries were designed to overcome that disability. However, changes in the perception of voters of the

roles of parties and candidates, and of the two Houses in the Parliament, also play an important role in determining the effectiveness of the electoral system.

HOUSE OF REPRESENTATIVES	SENATE
148 MPs	76 Senators
Each MP represents a separate electorate containing about 67 000 voters. N.S.W. has 51 electorates, Victoria 39, Queensland 24, W.A. and S.A. both 13, Tasmania 5, the A.C.T. 2 and the N.T. 1.	12 Senators are elected from each of the 6 States and 2 from each Territory.
MPs are elected for a term of 3 years.	Senators from the States are elected for 6-year terms, but half retire every 3 years. Those from the territories are elected for 3 years.
In each electorate, election is by preferential voting, one person being elected per electorate. Each candidate needs to win or obtain preferences of 50.1 % to be elected.	In each State, election is by proportional representation, usually 6 being elected at one time. A candidate then needs 13.9% of the vote for election.

CHAPTER 14

Electioneering

Most politicians never stop electioneering. The moment one election is finished, they begin analysing what went wrong or right, and making plans for the next election. Ministers and back-benchers and members of the Opposition organise their time so as to make the maximum political impact either on the voters as a whole or on the people living in their own particular electorate. Many of the things which politicians do—such as attending school fêtes or prize-givings, or local charity fund-raising—seem to the politicians to be required of them by their constituents as part of the price they pay for being the 'local Member'. They are functions which many politicians assume that they have to fulfil if they want to remain as the 'local Member' and be re-elected.

But electioneering takes over totally from everything else when the election date is announced and the Parliament's sittings end. This is when the politicians move completely into an 'election mode'. This is when political advertisements dominate radio and television, the party leaders deliver the policy speeches, and thunder everywhere around the country to try to persuade the voters to give them their support. This period of electioneering normally lasts from three to four weeks, though in 1984 it went on for almost eight weeks.

There can be little doubt that electioneering does have a significant effect on the outcome of any election. Voters are influenced by the policies which the parties produce and by the way the leaders stand up to the campaigns and to each other. Public opinion polls suggest that changes of 3 and 4 per cent can occur between the beginning of the election campaign period and polling day. More intensive studies show that a great many people do not finally decide how they will vote until the last few days before the election, and that many will swing from one side to the other during the campaign.

Policy speeches

The policy speeches by the party leaders are designed to form the basis of the whole election campaign. They contain the essential promises that the party is making to the electorate about its policies, together with the party's review of its own past performances and its critique of its opponents. The promises—whether they be tax cuts, or expenditure items—will not alter very much during the election campaign. Their total cost will be assessed on all sides, including by the media. This program of policy proposals (or mandate) which is contained in the policy speech is the basis on which the party seeks to gain election to Government. But the other parts of the policy speech—the political debate about the rights and wrongs of what has happened in the past, and the trustworthiness, or lack of it, of the people and parties contesting the current election—will change and develop during the campaign.

Normally, many weeks of work will have gone into the preparation of the campaign speech, particularly the determination of the particular set of policies on which the campaign is intended to be based. In the past, many of these decisions were taken just by the party leader, but in recent years responsibility for the content of policy speeches has been spread over the party's leadership and its campaign committee which will include members of its party machine who are not Members of Parliament. The rhetoric—the way the speech is written and delivered—is very much the responsibility of the leader, however.

The means of delivering the speech has changed also. Once, the speech was delivered to a large meeting, being broadcast simultaneously on radio, and then on television. More recently, political leaders have preferred to pre-record their television presentation, generally in front of a selected audience. Occasionally a leader has preferred a solo performance in a television studio, backed by pre-recorded material which is inserted to try to break the monotony of a long speech direct to the camera. But the speeches are also delivered to a live daytime audience, many hours before the television version is seen by most of the public. And some of the key parts of the speech will have been selectively 'leaked' to the Press, to make sure that the maximum 'exposure' is given to the party policy.

The content of the speech will reflect not only the party's

general policies and its attitudes to the current economic and international situations, but also its reading of the current political situation. This will be based on extensive surveys by public opinion experts to try to discover which issues are considered most important by the public, and the popularity of various policies and politicians. The findings by the pollsters will not necessarily influence the policies which the party will present to the public, but they may well affect the way in which those policies are presented.

Campaigning

The policy speech is delivered by the party leader and the campaign focus remains on him until polling day. He and his campaign staff will have drawn up an itinerary intended to take him to every State capital city and to every crucial swinging electorate. The itineraries of other leading figures in the party will have been arranged at the same time to ensure that they are spread out over as much of the country as possible, and that they visit the areas which are expected to be the most decisive in the election. But while a great deal of travelling is done, the emphasis is on exposure on television and, to a lesser extent, radio. Public meetings, which used to dominate the campaign period, have become unimportant except as a means of obtaining television coverage. Whereas the political leaders of the 1950s, 1960s and 1970s would have expected to hold at least a dozen and up to twenty major public meetings during an election campaign, the 1984 campaign resulted in each of the leaders holding only one or two evening meetings, and a few more daytime ones. This is partly because of an evaluation of the time and effort which needs to be put into an evening meeting in some suburban town hall, which will result in an audience of perhaps two thousand, as against the exposure to millions that the leader will get from talking with a television journalist for five minutes during the day. The increasing popularity of morning current affairs television programs means that the leaders now have to be available at about dawn for a series of interviews—a further reason for not having an exhausting meeting the night before.

The needs of the media tend to dominate the campaign of the leaders and their main deputies. It is only through the media that the leaders can reach the vast bulk of the voters. The media provide the only channel of communication—sometimes a two-way channel on talk-back radio, though the party faithful tend to dominate many shows. While the leaders will visit all capitals, they spend more time in Sydney and Melbourne than elsewhere, not just because those cities have most of the population within reach, but also because from them the politicians know that the commercial television networks will carry their messages through to all the other major population centres.

While the metropolitan media focus on the party leaders, a great deal of work is done at the local electorate level by those candidates who are not caught up in the national campaign. The highlight for a backbencher in a marginal electorate will be a visit from one of the party leaders, and every effort will be made to get him or her into all the local media outlets—the suburban or country paper, the local radio and television stations—and to have them seen in the company of the local candidate by as many people as possible. This may happen through a formal public meeting, through a meeting or walk through a shopping centre, or at the local railway station. Depending on the party and the electorate, the candidate may also try to organise a meeting at local factories, or a lunch with local businessmen.

The local campaign is normally controlled by the party's campaign director, not the candidate. The director tells the candidate what functions to attend, where he should hand out campaign literature, and what interviews he should give to the local media. He decides where and when to hold meetings at shopping centres and other areas where the use of a loud hailer will allow the candidate to make himself heard by at least some of his potential voters. The director is usually responsible for organising pamphlets and posters, and for having them put in mail boxes or pasted up around the electorate. The candidate's main job is to be available as required, to talk and make speeches, to sign letters and be friendly to all. His main electioneering will in fact have been done during the period before the campaign proper began, when he should have made himself known (favourably!) to as many voters in his electorate as he could. This is not such a difficult task for an MP once he is elected, because he will be contacted by many hundreds of his voters each year for help in dealing with Government and the Public Service. This personal contact is thought to be worth 1 or 2 per cent more votes for a good sitting member, and even more if he is particularly keen and attractive. Parties trying to win such electorates from sitting MPs normally try to decide who their candidate will be as early as possible, to allow him to get out in the electorate with sufficient time before the election to become known. There is no doubt that

PARLY DOLL
DEMOCRAT
STATESMAN
OLD LABOR
NEW LABOR
OLD LIBERAL
NATIONAL
NEW LIBERAL
OLD LABOR
NEW LABOR (S.A)
LIBERAL (VIC.)
DEMOCRAT
NEW LABOR (N.S.W.)
QLD NATIONAL
NEW LABOR (VIC)
NEW LABOR (VIC.)
OLD LABOR
NATIONAL
OLD LABOR
DEMOCRAT.
PRYOR

all this local work has some effect. Voting patterns are never uniform across the whole of Australia, or even across a whole State, and the way people perceive their local candidate—and even that they know who he is—is one of the factors which affect the way some electorates deviate from the average swings which occur.

Because voting is compulsory in Australian elections, the political parties do not have to worry about 'getting out the vote'. They may spend a little time organising transport to the polls for a few people on election day, but they do not have to devote very much attention to this problem. Instead, most local campaigns are concerned about organising postal and absent votes for people who will not be able to go to the polling booths, and particularly for people in hospitals, nursing homes, and old people's homes.

Advertising

The major parties put a great deal of reliance on their media advertising during the campaign period, both to try to get their own messages across, and to stop their opponents from dominating the scene. These advertising campaigns are controlled by federal campaign committees and by the State party organisations. They are by far the most expensive aspect of the major party campaigns. Local electorates campaigns, including local advertising, might cost a major party $30 000 or $40 000 in a marginal electorate, but probably no more than $1.5 million for all local campaigns throughout Australia. Advertising at the national and State level, on radio and television, and in the press, will probably cost two or three times that amount.

To get value for their money, the parties spend a lot of time and effort trying to ensure that they get the right message across to the right people. The political message is packaged in the same way as any other commercial product which might be advertised on television—partly because people expect to get advertising that way. Market research is used both before the advertisements are made and, if possible, while they are being used—though the comparative shortness of the campaign period limits the extent to which an advertising campaign can be changed in mid-stream. When it is changed, it is usually on the basis of the experience of the politicians and party bureaucrats, rather than as a result of adverse research findings.

Public funding

The ABC provides free time on radio and television to all the parties which are represented in Parliament, the amount of time roughly representing the level of voting support the party enjoys. But most radio and television time on the commercial stations and channels has to be paid for. This means that the wealthier parties are able to do more advertising and, if their advertising is effective, presumably maintain their political dominance.

Funding is a perpetual problem for political parties. Parties can rarely expect their members to finance all their activities, particularly at election time. So the parties try very hard to obtain donations from outside bodies. The Liberal and National parties have a far easier job than other parties. They receive large donations from private industry and from individuals. The Labor Party's basic financial support comes from the trade union movement, and to a lesser extent from business. Smaller parties such as the Australian Democrats and the Nuclear Disarmament Party tend to rely more on donations raised from their members and from individuals who support their aims.

The results of this system are made apparent by the time actually bought by the various political parties for election advertising—details of which have been published regularly by the body responsible for monitoring broadcasting and television services in Australia, which is currently the Australian Broadcasting Tribunal. Responsibility for supervising election expenditures shifted, however, to the Electoral Commission from the time of the 1984 election.

Those figures showed a fairly consistent pattern over the past few decades. In the 1983 elections, for example, of the total time purchased nationally on commercial television stations throughout the election campaign period, the Australian Labor Party bought 36 per cent, the Liberal Party 37 per cent, the National Party 25 per cent, Senator Harradine 1 per cent, and the Australian Democrats less than 0.05 per cent. The distribution was slightly different on radio. Labor bought 31 per cent of the advertising time, the Liberals 47 per cent, the National Party 17 per cent, the Australian Democrats 1.5 per cent, and Senator Harradine 0.4 per cent.

The figures make it clear why the idea of public funding (that is, some form of financial contribution to all parties being made by the Commonwealth) has been supported by the Labor Party and smaller parties. The 1983 parliamentary inquiry into public funding split along party lines. The Labor Party and the Australian Democrats argued that elections should be decided on the quality of policies put forward, and not on the quantity of money that was available to promote particular policies. They also thought that it was in the interests of democracy that public funds should be used to remove the necessity or the temptation to seek funds from sources who might impose conditions or require favours—in other words to prevent possible political corruption and the buying of political influence. The Liberal and National Parties both opposed public funding. They argued that public funds should simply not be spent on supporting political parties, and that there were higher priorities for public expenditures. It was also thought that public funding would reduce voluntary work for parties and reduce membership participation. One of the significant factors in the decision to recommend public funding was that many western democratic countries, including the United States, West Germany and Japan, have adopted public funding, and it has been introduced into New South Wales as well.

The committee majority recommended, and the Parliament adopted, a system of public funding which came into effect at the 1984 elections. Each party is entitled to 60 cents for each vote it receives in a House of Representatives election, and 30 cents for each Senate election vote, when the two elections are held at the same time. In a separate Senate election, each vote is worth 45 cents. The amount chosen was based on the fact that the basic postage rate at the time was 30 cents, but the actual amount is to be automatically increased with inflation. To qualify for public funding, a party would have to get at least 4 per cent of the vote. The total cost, per election, was expected to be about $7 million (at 1983 costs and enrolments).

The effect of public funding on the 1984 election is difficult to assess because the survey by the Electoral Commission of expenditures by political parties on radio and television advertising did not take in the whole of the 8-week election campaign, but only the time from the issue of the writs to the day of the election—about 5 weeks. In that period Labor's share of national electronic media advertising was 38 per cent, the Liberal Party's was 42 per cent, and the National Party's 19 per cent. The Australian Democrats spent about 0.7 per cent of the total, and other parties and independents a very small amount. Despite the fact that the survey does not cover the weeks immediately preceding and following the delivery of the campaign speeches, when there was a large amount of television and radio advertising, the total amount spent in the survey period was about $4.5 million, the highest amount ever spent on such advertising in an election. In 1983 the total spending was $4.325 million, in 1980 $2.759 million, in 1977 $2.109 million, and in 1975 $2.318 million. At the time of writing, insufficient data were available through returns to the Electoral Commission to allow any proper evaluation of the impact of public funding on the conduct of the various party campaigns.

What was clear, however, that the boost to party funds for campaigning would not result in the various parties dropping their own attempts to raise funds from their supporters, funds which would be used for party purposes between elections as well as for supplementing election campaign funds.

CHAPTER 15

Parliament House

Parliament has been a long time waiting for a permanent home.

When the first Commonwealth Parliament met, there was no national capital, or even any agreement as to where it should be. Those who negotiated the federation of the Australian colonies were afflicted by the rivalry between the two great cities of the time—Sydney and Melbourne. Those rivalries were such that there was no possibility of either of those cities becoming the capital of Australia, and so, following the example of the United States, it was decided that there should be a new national capital created in its own Territory, which would be cut out of one of the States. The Sydney–Melbourne rivalry again dictated that it should be somewhere between those places, and not too close to either. They wrote in the Constitution that

'The seat of Government of the Commonwealth shall be determined by the Parliament; and shall be within territory which shall have been granted to or acquired by the Commonwealth, and shall be vested in and belong to the Commonwealth, and shall be in the State of New South Wales, and be distant not less than one hundred miles from Sydney.

Such territory shall contain an area of not less than one hundred square miles. . .

The Parliament shall sit at Melbourne until it meet at the seat of Government.' (Section 125)

The search for the new capital territory began even before the Constitution was proclaimed, but it was not until after numerous inquiries and one false start (in 1904 the Parliament decided the territory should be around Dalgety, near the Victorian border) that the Commonwealth and New South Wales Parliaments agreed in 1909 on the eventual site of the new capital and the extent of its territory of 910 square miles, and not until 1911 that the Commonwealth finally took possession of it. Two years later the capital was named Canberra, in a ceremony held at a site between the present Parliament House and the new building for the Parliament. It took many years before a tentative beginning was made on the implementation of the plan drawn by Walter Burley Griffin, who won a world-wide competition to design the new capital. It was not until 1923 that work began on a temporary Parliament House, which was intended to house the Parliament for a maximum of fifty years. The Parliament moved from its interim residence in the Victorian Parliament in Melbourne to its temporary home below Camp Hill in Canberra in 1927, where it was to remain for sixty-one years.

The original buildings cost £650 000 but numerous extensions proved to be necessary to accommodate a greater than anticipated use of the building by Ministers (who preferred it to the more spacious rooms allocated to them in the various departments), increases in the number of Ministers, increases in the number of members in 1949 and 1985 (the last accommodated in an extension built in the sporting grounds provided for the Parliament, and connected to it by a first-floor walkway over one of the roads surrounding the original building) and the need for increased facilities and staff.

As it now exists, the three-storey building provides for:

- the chambers in which the House of Representatives and the Senate sit;
- accommodation for committees of the Parliament and of the various parliamentary political parties;
- a central reception hall for use by the public, and some other display areas for public information purposes, and public facilities such as a post office;
- offices for Ministers and their staffs;
- offices for the parliamentary officers, such as the Speaker and President, and the party whips;
- offices for all MPs and Senators into which some of them crowd their research assistant;
- offices and facilities for the various Parliament House departments, such as *Hansard* and the Library, though not all the Parliament House staff can be accommodated in Parliament House itself—many are in nearby buildings such as the Kurrajong Hotel, which was built originally to provide accommodation for parliamentarians and parliamentary staff;
- refreshment rooms and bars, and sporting facilities for parliamentarians and staff;

● accommodation for members of the media in offices in the Press Gallery.

The allocation of space in the old building is related more to the time when extensions were made, and particular needs developed, than to logical arrangement. Ministers' offices, for example, are scattered throughout the building, in odd groupings. Committee rooms, for which a need developed in the early 1970s, have often resulted from the amalgamation and conversion of rooms designed for other purposes.

The main ceremonial and functional rooms are located at the front of the middle floor. Steps from the central entrance lead up into King's Hall, the main public area, which is also used on formal occasions for ceremonials. To the left is the chamber of the House of Representatives, while the Senate chamber is immediately opposite it, on the right of King's Hall. The Speaker's Chair is at one end of a line drawn through the House of Representatives, across King's Hall and through the centre of the Senate to the President's Chair. If the doors into King's Hall were opened, the Speaker would be sitting looking down the centre of the House across King's Hall, at the President at the far end of his Senate Chamber.

Traditionally, the Government sits to the right of the presiding officer, the Opposition to the left, and independents and those belonging to smaller parties on the 'cross-benches' between them. Strictly speaking there are no cross-benches in the Australian Parliament because the seating is arranged in a somewhat elongated semicircle. In fact, when a Government has a very large majority, its members will occupy seats extending around the top of that ellipse on to what seems to be the Opposition side of the Parliament.

But the fact that the two chambers are arranged facing each other means that the Government benches of the House of Representatives are on the front, northern side of Parliament House, while the Government sits on the southern side of the Senate chamber. This somewhat complicates the arrangements of offices around the two chambers. It also means that walking from the Government or Opposition lobbies (corridors) from one chamber to the other involves crossing diagonally across King's Hall.

Government and Opposition each are allocated large meeting rooms on their respective sides of the two chambers, and the party leaders in both the House and the Senate have their offices close by. The Opposition leaders are directly in front of the lobby entrance to their particular House, while the Government leaders have corner suites. The Speaker and the President also have offices very close to their respective chambers, with space for their personal staffs, and for providing entertainment. In the case of the President, this has to include facilities for entertaining the person who opens the Parliament—usually the Governor-General, but on occasions the Queen.

The other people who need to have their offices immediately next to the chambers are the whips and the most senior parliamentary officials, the Clerks. The main whips' offices are located in recesses next to the chambers, between the lobbies and the chambers. They have direct access to the chambers to carry out their official duties of mustering their respective members. The Clerks have their offices in the corridors which run behind their chambers, and very close to the offices of the Speaker or President.

The Leader of the Government in the House of Representatives—the Prime Minister—has both a large set of offices to accommodate most (but not all) of his staff, and the facilities associated with the work of the Cabinet—a large meeting room, and a small ante-room and office.

Some of the Ministers have their offices close to the chambers, though the only one who needs to be close by is the Leader of the House. The others are scattered throughout the building, mainly in the newer areas where special ministerial suites have been built. Those suites normally contain a moderately sized office for the Minister, an office for his private secretary, a reception area staffed by a telephonist, and a room in which the remainder of the staff, perhaps a departmental official and several typists, will be located.

Individual Members and Senators get a one-room office, which they may share with a secretary or researcher, if they base a member of their staff in Canberra. However, attaining that one room has not always been easy. For many years in the 1950s, 1960s and 1970s, many members had to share rooms. This was never a satisfactory way to accommodate individual MPs. It was this accommodation pressure, together with the increasing needs of Ministers for adequate facilities for their staffs, which led to the minor building boom which greatly expanded the old Parliament House, and made it inevitable that the old idea of building a new and permanent Parliament would have to be taken up and carried through to fruition.

The services provided for MPs begin at the back of King's Hall, which opens into the Parliamentary Library. The front of the Library contains the latest newspapers published throughout

Australia—country and regional weekly papers as well as the metropolitan dailies. The main overseas papers are filed there as well, including several London and New York newspapers, along with the major newspapers from New Zealand, the Asian region and South Africa. Behind are reference books and even novels, and the library runs what is in effect a local library lending service for MPs and Senators, with access to the books of the National Library as well as its own substantial collection. Other library services—including the various research services, are available from here or from the continuation of the library on the ground floor of the building, or in various offices scattered throughout it. But many of the library staff have to be located outside the Parliament building, mainly in the former Kurrajong Hotel almost a kilometre away.

Behind the library, and reached by corridors from King's Hall and many other parts of the building, are the refreshment rooms—dining rooms for Members and Senators only, guest rooms for the use of parliamentarians, and several bars. On the ground floor there is a dining room and a separate bar for other parliamentary staff and workers in the Parliament, the 'non-members', as they are referred to.

On the top floor of the building near the two chambers are the rooms occupied by the parliamentary Press Gallery. Almost two hundred journalists, telex operators and their library staff are accommodated in rooms which comfortably would hold less than half that number. There are four television studios, and numerous rooms used for direct radio broadcasts. Many of the journalists are now directly connected to their newspapers by means of computer links—the journalists work on terminals which feed directly into the computers in Sydney and Melbourne of the major newspaper groups.

The new Parliament House was designed to provide a more logical arrangement of offices and functions, as well as ensuring that all the necessary facilities could be accommodated on the one site. The new Parliament will be contained in what is in essence a series of buildings or building elements. There are to be quite distinct and separate working environments for the main user groups—Members, Senators, the Ministry and their staff, the parliamentary support staff and the media. Altogether, the new Parliament House was designed to be about three and a half times the size of the 'temporary' building. The design chosen for the new site used the same basic idea of a three-storey building which was used in the original Canberra building for Parliament.

The geography of the present Parliament House has helped shape the way in which the Parliament itself has worked, and the relationship between the Parliament and the Government. The fact that the Prime Minister and his Ministers operate out of the Parliament building, rather than at separate establishments such as Number 10 Downing Street and Whitehall, in London, or the White House in Washington, is significant. Australian political leaders are far closer in physical terms to ordinary members of Parliament. They are more approachable to members of both sides of Parliament, and they are in fact approached more than their counterparts overseas. Whether the changed geography of the new Parliament will result in significant changes to the relationships which have developed between Government and Parliament in the old Parliament cannot be predicted. But there was certainly no intention that there should be changes. The briefs to the would-be architects of the new Parliament stressed the features of the present system, which was intended to be preserved. The judges who determined the architect for the new Parliament said that the winning design 'takes note of the functional layout of the provisional Parliament House, which has been strenuously tested and much developed in its evolution since 1927' (when it was first occupied). They were also confident of the symbolic success of the new design—that it met their criteria that 'The building must express in a symbolic way the unique national qualities, attributes, attitudes, aspirations and achievements of Australia. It must at the same time express an architectural identity, integrity and prominence consistent with its surroundings and the significance of the Parliament House'. The old Parliament House had comparatively few of those attributes. But it has helped to produce a workable form of parliamentary democracy.

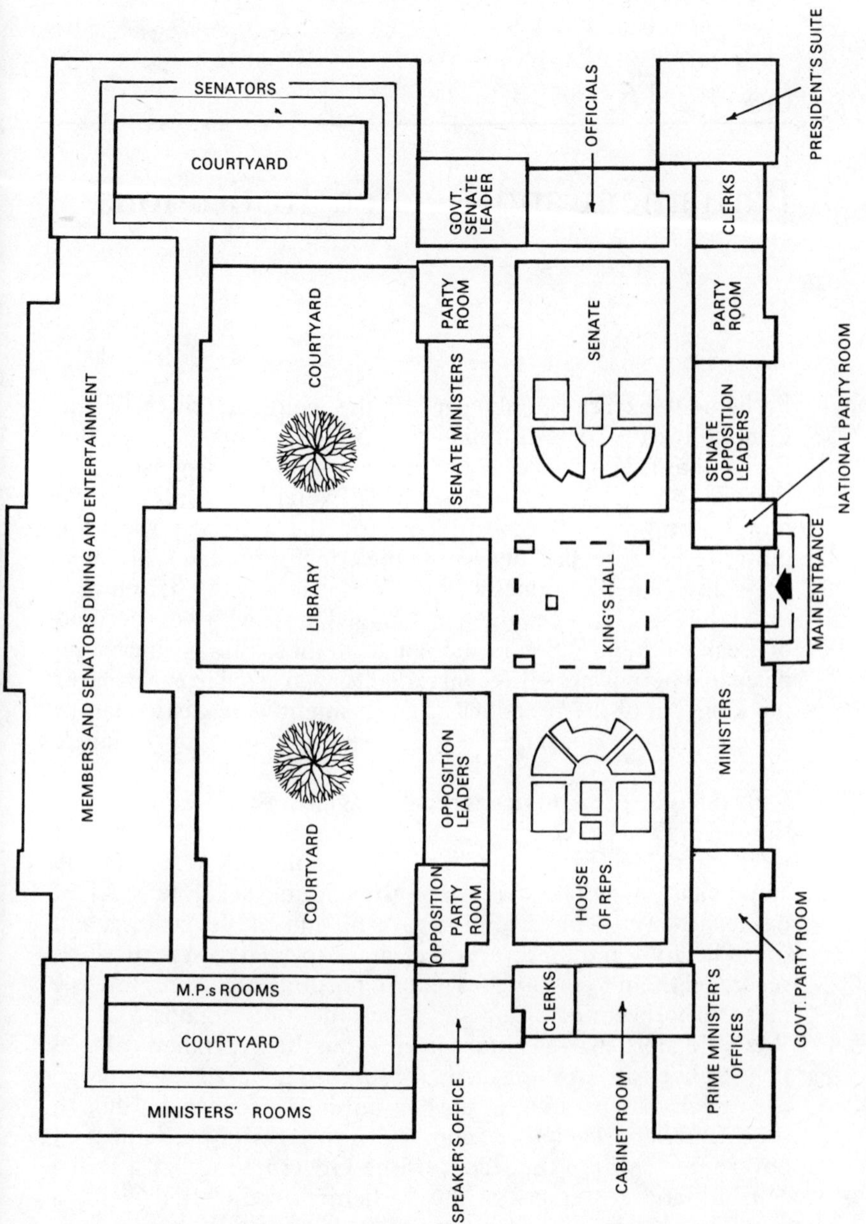

Details of Parliament House main floor plan

CHAPTER 16

Parliament and Related Institutions

Parliament exercises only part of the political power of the Commonwealth of Australia—the power to make laws. But Parliament is also concerned with the two other major aspects of the ways the power of the nation is exercised—the executive power (the power of government) and the judicial power (the power to interpret and determine meaning of the law). All these powers were held originally by the king. He was the person who made the laws, enforced them and judged those who were accused of breaking them. When he did not do all those things himself, he delegated his powers to his own servants, who acted in the name of the king. All of the functions of government were carried out in the name of the king, and the courts were controlled by the king's judges.

By the time the Americans revolted against British rule towards the end of the 18th century, ideas about the notion of government were changing. In England the king could still rule, but the Americans saw that there were three quite separate arms of national power—the executive government, the legislature, and the judiciary—and they were determined to create a system which separated them to the greatest extent possible, regarding this as a means of preventing autocratic government or dictatorship.

A little more than a century later, when the Australian colonial politicians began working on their proposed national constitution, the notion of separation of powers still held firm. And although the Australians wanted to adopt a British form of parliamentary government, where the leader of the Government was a Prime Minister and a Member of the Parliament rather than being a president elected in some other way, they still wrote their Constitution in such a way as to show they favoured the concept of the separation of powers. They in fact divided the Constitution into eight 'chapters'. The first, and by far the longest, deals with the Parliament and its powers. The second is concerned with the executive Government. The third deals with the Judicature. The others deal with finance and trade (the prime concern of many who wrote the Constitution); the States; new States; miscellaneous; and altering the Constitution.

The Executive Government

Executive power—which includes the power to run the public service and the defence forces, as well as the ability to determine national policies which do not have to be implemented by legislation—is given by the Constitution to the Queen, though the Constitution itself specifies that that power is to be exercised by the Governor-General. He in turn is normally required to act with the advice of a Federal Executive Council. This Council consists of Ministers of State, who cannot hold office for more than three months without being or becoming Members of the federal Parliament. So although a separate executive government is created by the Constitution, that same document effectively eliminates a complete separation of the executive power from the legislative power by requiring that the Ministers who in fact exercise the powers of government must be Members of the Parliament. The ramifications and implications of that relationship are discussed in more detail in Chapter 18.

The Queen and the Governor-General

Australia is a monarchy. The Queen's position as head of state is firmly declared in the Constitution. Members of Parliament are required by the Constitution to swear or affirm that they 'will be faithful and give true allegiance to' the present Queen or King before taking their place in the Parliament. And although the Parliament has passed an Act providing that the Monarch is Queen of Australia, the Constitution makes it clear that it is the King or Queen of the United Kingdom who is the head of State in Australia.

The Queen is an essential part of the constitutional definition of the Parliament. The Federal Parliament 'shall consist of the Queen, a Senate, and a House of Representatives' (Section 1 of the Constitution). But the Queen's powers, both as a part of that Parliament and as head of the executive government, are mostly given to the Governor-General. Those that she retains, such as the power to disallow any law within one year of its assent by the Governor-General, are essentially dead letters. They have never been used, and there is never likely to be an occasion now when they would be used.

The same is not true of some of the powers given to the Governor-General, as the constitutional crisis of 1975 demonstrated. The Constitution gives the Governor-General a very large number of powers. Many of those powers are stated by the constitution to be used only with the advice of the executive council—the Ministers of the elected Government. But many others contain no such qualification. In 1975 Sir John Kerr, as Governor-General, was able to rely on some of these powers and also on what he claimed to be his inherent powers as Governor-General to dismiss the elected Government of the day. He also was able to ignore the House of Representatives, which passed a motion of no confidence in the Government he appointed, by the simple expedient of not receiving the Speaker of the House of Representatives. But he was able to do those things because he was in a position to quickly dissolve both the Houses of Parliament and to require an election to be held. Given the current state of public opinion, it was inevitable that his action would be effectively endorsed through the defeat of the party which he sacked from Government. However, the storm which arose over his action makes it highly unlikely that any future Governor-General would seek to exercise similar powers.

This means that the Governor-General has few powers which he can exercise independently of the elected Government, but those few he has are of considerable importance. One of the most important is the power of the Governor-General to determine whether he will grant a double dissolution of both Houses of the Parliament if he is requested to do so by the Prime Minister. There are now sufficient precedents (there have been five double dissolutions), backed by judgments of the High Court, to suggest that the granting of such a request is almost inevitable. But the matter is not completely cut and dried, as Mr Fraser discovered when, as Prime Minister, he sought a double dissolution in 1983. The Governor-General not only required time to read at his convenience all the material supplied to him by the Prime Minister, but also invited a further explanation in writing before he was satisfied that the necessary conditions for a double dissolution existed. After a telephone conversation and a second letter from Mr Fraser, the Governor-General wrote back to him saying,'As a result of your second letter to me, in which you speak of difficulties of the immediate past and describe a double dissolution as critical to the workings of the Government and of the Parliament, I am now satisfied that in accordance with your advice I should dissolve the Senate and the House of Representatives simultaneously. . .'

Another time when the powers of a Governor-General would be important would be in the event of a political crisis following the breakdown of a coalition Government, or a factional fight within a governing party. If there were a split in a party which was in Government, for example, it might be necessary for the Governor-General to decide whether he would grant a Prime Minister an election if he were to ask for one. Essentially, the Governor-General has to determine which party or which person controls a majority of votes in the House of Representatives—and he might insist that any political problem should first be thrown into that House for it to attempt a resolution. Otherwise he might be seen as taking sides in a factional or coalition dispute. The Governor-General is the Queen's Australian representative, but for more than fifty years it has been the Australian Government, rather than the British Government and/or the Queen, which has effectively chosen the person who is to fill the position of Governor-General. Governors-General usually hold office for five-year terms. It is then the Prime Minister of the day who communicates with the Palace in London to negotiate the next holder of the office.

But the Parliament has no say in the choice of the Governor-General, and has no ability to have him replaced. Its only power over the Governor-General is to decide what his salary should be. To prevent the Parliament indirectly influencing what the Governor-General does, the Constitution requires the salary for a Governor-General to be laid down before he takes up his post.

The Governor-General has quite direct powers over the Parliament, however. He can dissolve the House of Representatives at any time, and, under circumstances laid down by the Constitution, can dissolve both Houses of Parliament. Before the Parliament can pass any law to spend money, it must have a message from the Governor-General specifying the amount required and its purpose (this is done in a single-sentence message which is read to the House of Representatives during the passage of the legislation).

These powers stress the apparent separation of the functions of the Parliament and the executive. Just how separate they are depends on the will of the Parliament and the executive. The trend these days is to keep the executive as close to the Parliament as possible.

The High Court

The 'Judicature' section of the Constitution creates the High Court and gives the Parliament powers to create other federal courts and to give State courts the ability to determine such federal matters as are specified by the Parliament. There have in fact been several other federal courts created—currently there are the Federal Court (which hears disputes and prosecutions under the Trade Practices Act, and bankruptcy and arbitration matters) and the Family Court. Among the federal matters which come before State Courts are taxation appeals and charges under the Customs Act.

The High Court stands at the apex of the entire court system in Australia. It may hear appeals from all courts, State and federal, and in all matters, whether local, State or federal. It makes decisions based on its interpretation of federal, State or local laws, and according to its view of the 'common law', that part of the law which was inherited from English judge-made law and which has been adapted by the Australian courts, and upon which the High Court's view is conclusive.

The High Court's most significant function is to determine the meaning of the Constitution, a task it often has to face when there is a challenge to State or federal laws. The Constitution sets out the powers of the Federal Parliament, and the Parliament cannot make laws on matters outside those powers. If it attempts to do so, the High Court has the power to intervene (if it is called upon to do so by a State or someone directly affected by the 'law') and to declare that the particular law is not a law—that it was beyond the power of the Parliament to make such a law. The Constitution also says that when there are federal and State laws which are inconsistent, the federal law shall prevail (Section 109). This means that State laws can be challenged if they deal with the same subject-matter as a federal law in a manner which contradicts the federal law. State laws can also be ruled to be invalid if they stray into any of the areas which the Constitution says are the sole responsibility of the Commonwealth. (For example, the Commonwealth is given exclusive power over import duties and excises, and the High Court has ruled that most sales taxes are excises and therefore cannot be imposed by the States—though the States keep trying to find ways around this ban.)

The High Court as the interpreter of the Constitution insists on the division of powers between the Parliament, the executive and the judiciary which the Constitution seems to indicate. It has ruled that judges and judges alone may exercise judicial functions, but that judges cannot exercise administrative or legislative functions except when those functions are necessarily associated with their judicial work. The High Court has also insisted that Parliament should not interfere with the way the Court carries out its function as the interpreter of the Constitution. The Court has ruled that the Parliament cannot write into a law any particular facts which need to be determined by the Court when it has to decide whether a piece of legislation is constitutional or not. The extreme position

would be for the Parliament to write a law in which it declared that the law was valid because it fell within a constitutional power—the Court says Parliament cannot do that, or adopt any approach in which it attempts to avoid the full scrutiny by the Court of those elements which determine whether a law is valid or not. The most the Parliament can do is to explain in the Acts Interpretation Act what it means by various words which it uses in its legislation (for example, the word 'he' includes the word 'she') and also tell the Courts the type of material they may refer to in order to work out Parliament's intention in passing a particular law (the courts sometimes rely on what they think is the parliamentary intention if a law is worded ambiguously). Recently the federal Parliament decided that the courts could look at *Hansard* and at explanatory memoranda which are tabled with Bills, to help in the courts' understanding of the Parliament's intentions.

The terms and methods of appointment and dismissal of judges are dealt with by the Constitution (Section 72). High Court judges are appointed by the Governor-General in Council—which means that they are decided on by the federal Cabinet. Parliament, however, has passed a law to require the Government to 'consult' with the States before making any appointments to the High Court. But consultation does not give the States any kind of veto power, and the Parliament itself does not have the ability to prevent the appointment of a judge in the way, for example, that the American Senate is required to consent to any appointment to the United States Supreme Court.

Parliament also determines the size of the High Court. When it was established in 1903 the Court had three members. The Court was later increased to five and then to seven Justices, which is its present size. The Parliament also decides what salaries and allowances the Justices should get, though it has largely delegated this to the Remuneration Tribunal. It also has the power to remove judges from office, though only 'on the ground of proved misbehaviour or incapacity' by means of an address by both Houses of Parliament addressed to the Governor-General in Council. The Constitution sets the retiring age for judges at seventy, though before it was amended in 1977, the Constitution required judges to be appointed for life.

The High Court plays an extremely important role in national political affairs because of its duty to interpret the Constitution and to maintain the balance between federal and State Parliaments. That role requires it to be independent of the federal Parliament, an independence which is guaranteed to it by the constitutional separation of power. When the Court makes a decision which declares that an attempt by the Parliament to make a particular law has failed, or that a particular law does not in fact say what the Parliament or the Minister thought it was supposed to say, the political consequences can be quite significant. For a decade, for example, the High Court interpreted a 'catch-all' section of the Income Tax Assessment Act in such a way that it was quite unable to catch tax evasion or avoidance. That put great pressure on the tax system as avoidance and evasion grew, and great political pressure on the federal Government. Federal–State financial relations have also been greatly affected by the Court's interpretation of several Sections of the Constitution which have had the effect of limiting State fund-raising and increasing the ability of the Commonwealth to dictate terms to the States on the way they spend moneys given by the Commonwealth. Another example is the way the Court has interpreted the 'free-trade' provision in the Constitution to prevent the nationalisation of banking (and presumably any other industry which has interstate ramifications). That decision makes the Labor Party's long-held ideal of nationalising industry totally impractical. At the same time it poses a threat to primary industry marketing schemes in which crops are automatically acquired by national or State marketing bodies such as the Wheat Board or the Queensland Barley Board, schemes which have been supported by all political parties. These examples demonstrate that what the High Court says may be based on legal principles, but it has important effects on the way political decisions are made, the nature of those decisions, and the relations between the Commonwealth and the State, and that the powers of the Parliament to deal with many of those political problems are in turn limited by what the Court says are the powers of the Parliament. The Commonwealth Parliament simply does not have the power to do many of the things which the Parliament (and perhaps even the people who elect it) would like it to do. And the High Court sits in judgment on the Parliament to ensure it does not go beyond its constitutional boundaries.

The States

The whole purpose of the Constitution is to separate the functions of government at two levels, national and State. The Australian Commonwealth would not have been created in 1901 had it not been for the fact that the founders were able to draw up a system which would preserve the integrity of the different colonies. Federalism was a condition of nationhood. Yet the colonies which became the new States had to surrender some of their powers—those which were specified in the Constitution (see Chapter 17). They also had to give up their independence because they realised how interdependent all of them were. They gave up such sovereignty as they had (they were all then subject to British legislation) for a guarantee in the Constitution which in Section 106 preserved their constitutions, subject to the Commonwealth Constitution, and all of the powers of their Parliaments and their laws, again subject to the provisions of the Commonwealth Constitution (Ss. 107–8). The boundaries of the States could not be altered without the permission of the State, and no constitutional alteration which would affect a State's representation in the federal Parliament, or its boundaries, could be passed without the people of the State approving it.

The separation of powers

Australia does not have a 'sovereign' Parliament or even 'sovereign' States (as some State politicians frequently claim). The British Parliament is sovereign in Britain because it is the supreme power in Britain. There is no constitution to deny it any powers or limit its functions. The Parliament at Westminster embodies the judicial as well as the legislative function (it is referred to sometimes as the High Court of Parliament, and a judicial committee of the House of Lords is in fact the ultimate court of appeal in Britain). And the executive is a part of the Parliament also and subject to its ultimate control, even though most of the time it is the executive which seems to control the Parliament. The Australian Parliament is in an entirely different situation. Its powers are limited by the Constitution. The exercise of its powers are reviewable by a Court over which it can exercise no control at all. And while most executive functions are in fact carried out through Ministers who are answerable to the Parliament, there are vital powers over the Parliament's very existence which are exercisable by the Governor-General, who is not answerable to the Parliament.

CHAPTER 17

Parliament and the Constitution

About half of the 128 Sections of the Commonwealth Constitution are devoted to matters concerning the federal Parliament, such as its composition, its election and its powers. This is the framework in which the Parliament operates, providing its structure and the outer limits of its legislative powers.

Powers

Because Australia is a federation of States, none of its Parliaments is sovereign or all-powerful. Each is confined to predetermined limits which are laid down in the constitutional compact which created Australia as a federal nation. The method of allocating powers between the federal Parliament and the State Parliaments which is used in the Australian Constitution is to specify the powers which the Commonwealth should have, and to say that everything else remains with the States. Some of the powers given to the Commonwealth are made exclusive—the States are forbidden to have any laws in those areas. But most of the powers given to the Commonwealth are made concurrent—the States are allowed to make laws about the same subjects, provided that they do not run into any conflict with federal laws. The Constitution says that in the event of any such conflict (inconsistency), the Commonwealth law prevails over the State law. This is so irrespective of whether the Commonwealth or the State made the law first. In fact the idea of having most of the Commonwealth's powers listed as concurrent rather than exclusive was to allow existing State laws to continue until such time as the Commonwealth got round to making laws for the whole nation on the particular issue. The Commonwealth, for example, is given powers over marriage and divorce, but there was no federal divorce law until 1959—before that time people in different States had quite different divorce laws. There are still some areas of possible Commonwealth power which the Commonwealth has not fully used.

These concurrent powers are the main powers used by the Federal Parliament. They are listed in Section 51 of the Constitution as forty separate items. One of these was added by a Constitutional amendment in 1946, and this gave the Commonwealth power to provide a whole range of pensions and benefits, such as to widows and students, and for medical, dental and hospital services, which were simply not envisaged by the original founders of the Constitution who made provision only for the payment of invalid and old-age pensions. A second alteration to these powers was made by a referendum in 1967 which altered a Section which gave the Commonwealth powers to make 'special' laws for the people of any race. The original grant of power stopped the Commonwealth making special laws for Aborigines, but that prohibition was deleted by the 1967 amendment.

Among the powers listed under Section 51 of the Constitution are: taxation; currency; quarantine; weights and measures; bankruptcy and insolvency; marriage; immigration and emigration; the influx of criminals; external affairs; the naval and military defence of the Commonwealth (in 1900 no one was thinking ahead to the possibility of air defence); borrowing money on the public credit of the Commonwealth; and trade and commerce with other countries and among the States. Most of them are not as simple or straight-forward as they seem, and many have been the subject of interpretation by the High Court.

The Court has several times had to decide what powers the Commonwealth can exercise under the heading 'external affairs'. During the 1980s the Court decided that the 'external affairs' power gave the Commonwealth Parliament power to implement genuine international treaties which Australia had signed and agreed to abide by. Fulfilling the obligations of those treaties might involve legislation which would go beyond the normal bounds of Commonwealth power, and allow the Commonwealth to interfere with what would otherwise be functions or laws of the States. But because the laws were part of the Commonwealth's conduct of its external affairs, and could affect its relations with other countries if it did not carry out its treaty obligations, the Court held that the Commonwealth did have the power to completely implement those treaties. The two treaties which came directly before the Court were the International Convention on the Elimination of All Forms of Racial Discrimination and the

World Heritage Convention. The first provided the basis for the Commonwealth Parliament to pass the *Racial Discrimination Act 1975*, while the second was the basis of legislation in 1983 to protect the Tasmanian wilderness area and prevent the Tasmanian Government from building the Franklin Dam.

Not all the Commonwealth's powers have been interpreted by the Court so expansively. One of the items in Section 51 gives the Commonwealth power to make laws 'with respect to conciliation and arbitration for the prevention and settlement of industrial disputes extending beyond the limits of any one State'. This does not give the Commonwealth power to make laws to settle strikes or to fix wages or working conditions. All it does is give the Commonwealth power to establish a body which will provide arbitration and/or conciliation. That body can then only deal with 'industrial disputes', a term which until recently has meant disputes concerning industry, and for a long time the Court said that firefighters or teachers were not an 'industry' and therefore could not be covered by federal awards—an award being a decision of the conciliation and arbitration commission. The clause also specifies that there has to be an interstate dispute before the Commonwealth body can take an interest in it, but there does not have to be an actual strike to create this dispute, because the court has held that the making and rejection of a claim, on paper, is enough to create a dispute.

The Court has allowed a natural extension of some of the words of the Constitution to allow the Commonwealth to cope with concepts which the original makers of the Constitution knew nothing about. For example, the Constitution gives the Commonwealth power to make laws with respect to 'postal, telegraphic, telephonic, and other like services'. That power has been used as the basis of the Commonwealth's legislation controlling the licensing of radio and television broadcasting.

But the scope of other powers has been changed by nothing more nor less than changes in the attitude of the High Court. In 1906, for example, the Parliament passed a law to control monopolies and other restrictive trade practices, under that part of Section 51 which gives the power to make laws with respect to 'foreign corporations, and trading or financial corporations formed within the limits of the Commonwealth'. The High Court held that law was invalid. But more than half a century later the Court changed its mind, opening the way to a vast network of laws designed to provide uniform consumer protection laws (in addition to State laws on the same subject) and trade practices legislation.

The number of powers over which the Commonwealth has exclusive control is much smaller. Section 52 lists just three—power over the seat of Government (the Australian Capital Territory) and all places acquired by the Commonwealth for public purposes; matters relating to the Commonwealth Public Service; and other matters declared by the Constitution to be within the Commonwealth's exclusive power. That last category includes the power under Section 90 to control customs, excise and bounties.

But there are other powers too which are scattered throughout the Constitution—power to make laws concerning federal elections; powers concerning the way the judicature is organised and in relation to the jurisdiction of the High Court, and to create new federal courts. Perhaps the most important of these additional powers is contained in Section 96 of the Constitution which allows the Parliament to 'grant financial assistance to any State on such terms and conditions as the Parliament thinks fit'. This power has resulted in an enormous increase in the range of matters in which the Federal Parliament takes an interest—areas certainly not contemplated when the Constitution was written. Under the grants power, the Commonwealth has come to dominate the funding of education throughout Australia, including the determination of policies for universities and other tertiary institutions such as colleges, though the Constitution gives the Commonwealth Parliament no general power over education. A similar situation has occurred in road construction, public housing and health and hospital services.

Freedoms

Unlike the position in the United States, the Australian Constitution contains no Bill of Rights providing fundamental constitutional guarantees of various freedoms. This absence is in accordance with the standard British approach that such freedoms as are appropriate are provided under the ordinary law. British and Australian law provides no equivalent freedom to the guarantee of freedom of the press and other civil freedoms enumerated in the American Constitution. Nor is there in Australia a guarantee of equality of political rights, as is provided in the United States Constitution.

There are, however, several fundamental guarantees in the Australian Constitution which cover part of the area of basic freedoms. The power given to the Commonwealth in Section 51 (xxxi) to acquire property is accompanied by the qualification that the acquisition must be on 'just terms'. Section 80 requires that there should be trial by jury for any indictment of an offence against Commonwealth law. Section 116 says that the Commonwealth should not make any law for establishing any religion, or imposing any religious observance, or any religious test for a public office, or prohibiting the free exercise of any religion. Section 92 of the Constitution says that trade, commerce and intercourse between the States shall be absolutely free, and this has been interpreted as preventing any nationalisation of private industry.

Relations between the Houses of Parliament

The Constitution gives the House of Representatives and the Senate almost equal powers in relation to legislation, with the balance slightly tipped in favour of the House of Representatives, which is clearly intended to be the Chamber where Governments are formed or defeated. But at the same time the Constitution gives the Senate immense political power. The Constitution provides only one 'ultimate' solution to conflict between the two Houses—a dissolution of both. But in many cases that answer is far too drastic. The fact that there is no flexibility in solving deadlocks between the Houses has helped to make political conflict worse than it might otherwise be.

The powers of the two Houses are dealt with primarily in Section 53 of the Constitution, which concludes with the statement, 'Except as provided in this Section, the Senate shall have equal power with the House of Representatives in respect of all proposed laws'. The main differences spelt out in the Section are:

● Bills which impose taxes or provide for the spending of money can only be introduced into the House of Representatives;
● The Senate cannot amend bills imposing taxes, or those which appropriate money for ordinary government services;
● The Senate cannot amend any Bill in such a way that it would increase any proposed charge or burden on the people.

But these limitations on the Senate's power are made insignificant by another provision of the same Section of the Constitution which spells out the Senate's right to request amendments or deletions from any of the Bills which it is not allowed to amend of its own power. The Senate has demonstrated repeatedly that the power to request amendments is effectively the same as the power to make amendments. The Senate can simply go on making requests, just as it can go on making amendments, in relation to other legislation, until the House of Representatives either agrees with it, or refuses to proceed further with the legislation, or until the Senate itself decides not to persist with the request or the amendment. For the unstated but clearly inferred power which the Senate retains is its ability to reject any legislation, or to refuse to pass it (which amounts to the same thing). This means that although the Constitution lists a series of apparent limitations on the Senate's power, they do not prevent the Senate from demanding that its views be taken into account, because it always has the ultimate power to reject any law, including any financial, tax, money, Budget or Supply Bill.

The Senate is given the political power to resist the pressures of the Government and the House of Representatives and to insist on its view in relation to amendments or to the general thrust of legislation, by several provisions of the Constitution which relate to the Senate's structure. Firstly, the Senate is an elected Chamber, like the House of Representatives. Although it does not represent people in proportion to population, but does so according to the State they live in, the Senate is made up of people who are democratically elected. Senators can claim an independent mandate from the people, a mandate to do something different from what the Government claims it has a mandate to do. In Britain the House of Commons was able to reduce the powers of the House of Lords to such an extent that the Lords is now able to do little more than delay the passage of laws on which the Commons insists. But that process was possible because the Lords was an undemocratic Chamber, in no sense representative of the people, which never faced an election to provide it with any sort of popular legitimacy. And the Lords did not have the protection enjoyed by the Senate of a written Constitution which is extremely difficult to change.

A second factor giving the Senate political power is the fact that Senators generally are elected for six-year terms (twice that of Members of the House of Representatives) and the Government cannot force the Senate to premature elections (except in a double dissolution).

Double dissolutions

Section 57 of the Constitution is the only means made available by the Constitution for the settlement of disputes between the two Houses of Parliament. It gives the Government an option of taking the drastic move of having the House and the whole of the

Senate face an election together, provided that certain conditions are satisfied:

- the Senate has to reject or fail to pass, or pass with amendments which are unsatisfactory to the House, a law proposed by the House of Representatives;
- at least three months later, the House has to put forward the same proposed law, and once again the Senate has to reject it, or fail to pass it, or pass it with amendments which the House will not agree to.

'Fails to pass' can mean many things, including a decision by the Senate to send a Bill off for a committee investigation, provided it seems that the Senate is not following normal procedure and seems to want to avoid passing the Bill.

The fact that a Bill is rejected by the Senate in the way necessary to satisfy the requirements of this Section does not mean that the Prime Minister has to go to the Governor-General to ask for a double dissolution. In fact a Prime Minister can save up a series of Bills which satisfy the Section and get a double dissolution to cover all of them. The only constitutional limitation is that he cannot seek a double dissolution within six months of the time an ordinary election would normally be due. Of course he will also have political limitations—such as the state of public opinion, the type of legislation which has been rejected by the Senate, and the prospects that the Government might have of changing the Senate situation as a result of the election.

If a Government wins a double dissolution but still cannot get the Senate to pass the Bills which were the basis of the double dissolution, it can then hold a joint sitting of the two Houses to vote on them. Though there have been five double dissolutions (in 1914, 1951, 1974, 1975 and 1983) there has only been one such joint sitting of the House and Senate, in 1974, to pass double dissolution Bills. In 1914 and 1983 the Government of the day was defeated in the double dissolution election, while in 1951 the Government of the day retained office and also won control of the Senate. In 1975 the double dissolution was tied up with the dismissal of the Whitlam Government and the Fraser Government had no wish to pass the Bills on which, in theory, it was granted the election.

Changing the Constitution

The Constitution provides just one way in which its terms and provisions may be changed: first, legislation setting out the proposed amendment has to be passed through the Parliament (or in certain circumstances, just one House of the Parliament); then the proposed amendment has to be put to a referendum at which all Australian electors have a vote. To be successful, a proposed amendment has to be approved by an overall majority of voters throughout Australia, AND it also has to win a majority of votes in four of the six States. Several referendums have been approved by a majority of voters but have failed the second hurdle—a majority of votes in a majority of States. But most referendums have simply failed to get public support. Only eight of the referendums put to the people between 1901 and 1984 have passed all the conditions laid down in the Constitution and thus become part of the Constitution. Most of these have been technical, non-contentious matters. Only two amendments involving a real increase in powers for the Commonwealth have been passed. One allowed the Commonwealth to pay various pensions and benefits to people and the other removed a discrimination against Aborigines.

Australians have tended to be very doubtful about making any changes to their Constitution, and this doubt has been played upon by all political parties when they have been in Opposition. A feature of referendums seeking increased powers for the Commonwealth has been that parties which have sought particular powers while in Government have advocated a 'no' vote when the other main political party has tried to introduce an amendment to obtain the very same powers.

At least three serious attempts have been made to try to achieve all-party political consensus in order to get the necessary support for what all sides see to be necessary reforms of the Constitution. A Royal Commission into the Constitution was held in the 1920s, an all-party Parliamentary Committee produced a series of reports in the 1950s, and in 1973 there began a 'Constitutional Convention' of Members of federal and State Parliaments of all parties, and representatives of local government, to try to work out an agreed non-partisan series of amendments to the Constitution. These meetings, every year or two, have produced some agreements, but these have mostly broken down when a Government has wanted to produce referendum proposals to put the proposals to the people for approval. In 1985 the Government announced that it would not persevere with the Conventions, but instead would establish a Constitutional Commission, to conduct a full review of the Constitution. It would present its proposals in mid-1988.

CHAPTER 18

Parliament and Government

Responsible government lies at the heart of the system of government used in Canberra and in all the States. It is a system which has developed over hundreds of years in England and been adapted elsewhere in democratic countries throughout the world. But its practice is made incredibly difficult when, as in Australia, it is melded with a federal system of government.

The problem arises because of a fundamental conflict between the requirements of the two systems. Responsible government is based on the notion that Ministers are responsible for their conduct of government to the House of Representatives. Federalism required the creation of an upper house which could resist the determinations of the House to which the Ministers—the Government—were responsible. The result is that Ministers and governments have what amounts to two sets of responsibilities which may be in conflict—responsibility to the House of Representatives, and responsibility to the Senate. Sometimes this may have what many people would regard as the desirable outcome of forcing Ministers to be very cautious and conservative in their activities. But it can also result in Governments being less able to govern properly and effectively. Commonwealth Governments are certainly more hamstrung in carrying out their policies than are the Governments of other countries, or the Governments of most of the States.

Nevertheless it is true to describe the system of government imposed by the Constitution as one of responsible government because it has the following features:
- the Government of the day is chosen from the party or parties which control a majority of Members in the House of Representatives;
- the Government is run by a group of Ministers who must be (or

become within three months) Members of Parliament or Senators (Constitution, Section 64);
- the Ministers control the activities of their respective Departments and are responsible to Parliament for their conduct;
- the House of Representatives controls the life of individual ministers or the Government as a whole—if it votes no confidence in a Minister he must resign; if it votes no confidence in the Government, or refuses to pass any significant legislation, the Government must either resign or call an election.

Ministerial responsibility

At the core of the concept of 'responsible government' is 'ministerial responsibility', a term which describes three different and distinct relationships or codes of conduct.

The first sense in which ministerial responsibility is used is to describe the relationship between the Governor-General and the elected Government of the day; the second concerns the relationship of individual Ministers to their colleagues in the Cabinet and to the Cabinet as a whole; and the third is to describe the relationship between Ministers and the House of Representatives.

Ministerial responsibility in relation to the Governor-General involves the theory that the Crown can do no wrong (a concept designed to protect the Crown). It means that any action taken by the Crown is either taken directly on the advice of 'responsible Ministers' (which is how the term 'ministerial responsibility' is involved) or alternatively that there is a group of responsible Ministers who will take responsibility for the action. This is why in 1975 the Governor-General could not just call an election in defiance of the wishes of the Whitlam Government; he had to sack that Government first and install a new Prime Minister who would take 'responsibility' for his action—a responsibility which has to be answered for at the ballot box. Responsible government in this sense means that there are always elected persons who take responsibility for the actions of Government, and that such actions are not to be sheeted home to people who are appointed (Governors-General or Governors) or who occupy their position through inheritance (the Queen or her successors).

The second manifestation of the notion of ministerial responsibility concerns the relationship between a Minister and his colleagues, both individually and collectively when they are the Cabinet. This is really concerned with the idea that the

Government is a single unit, and it is often referred to as 'cabinet solidarity' (and is really a formal way of expressing the idea that all the members of the Cabinet must sink or swim together). Decisions are taken either by individual Ministers or by the Cabinet as a whole, but in either eventuality all the members of the Government are bound by what is decided. A Government cannot have more than one policy on an issue, and individual members of the Government cannot distance themselves from a particular decision, or opt out of a course of action which the Government has determined.

The theory of Cabinet solidarity is faced with two strong Australian distortions. The first is provided when a Liberal–National coalition is in Government. Because the interests of the two parties are not always the same, some of the members of the Cabinet may sometimes make known their disapproval of a particular decision by the coalition Cabinet, for the sake of their relations with their own party members and/or for their own party's electoral advantage. A second concerns the Labor Party when in office. Labor Ministers and the Labor Cabinet are responsible to the party Caucus as a whole, and Ministers are able to appeal to the Caucus against decisions of the Cabinet. This was a problem for the Whitlam Government but less so for the Hawke Government whose Ministers agreed to be bound by Cabinet solidarity.

The third aspect of ministerial responsibility concerns the responsibility that individual Ministers have to the Parliament. Ministers are constitutionally responsible for the administration of their departments, though actual responsibility lies with the public servant who heads the department. Those public servants, however, have to answer to their Ministers. Ministers are liable to be questioned in the Parliament about any aspect of policy for which they are responsible and for any action taken by their departmental officers. They are responsible for those actions in the sense of being liable to be held to account for them (for example, by being censured) only in so far as it would be expected that the Minister himself should have known what was happening and permitted an erroneous decision or course of action. In parliamentary terms, the worst crime (to judge by the complaints which MPs and Senators have made over the years) is to have 'misled' (that is, lied to) the Parliament.

Ministers who make serious mistakes or who knowingly mislead Parliament are theoretically expected to resign. What occasionally happens is that a Minister who has made a political mess of a situation will offer his resignation to his Prime Minister, who will make a decision as to whether the resignation will be acepted on his evaluation of the political harm which may be done to the Government by not acknowledging the mistake. That will often depend more on the reaction of the media to the particular problem than to the reaction of the Members of the Parliament to whom the Minister is supposed to be responsible. And this is because the tight party system means that a Minister is in no danger of being censured in the House of Representatives, because his party controls a majority of votes there. A censure might be passed in the Senate (and has been on several occasions) but this has had no direct effect on the Minister continuing in office because of the idea that Governments (and Ministers) are made and unmade in the House of Representatives, not the Senate.

This does not mean that Ministers can ignore their duties to the House (or Senate). A Minister's relationship with the Parliament can be an important element in the general political situation, and in the Minister's standing within his own party. So that while Ministers are no longer liable to be forced from office by censure in the Parliament, their fate within their party and the political fate of their party, can be affected by their actions. While Ministers who make mistakes do occasionally resign in Australia, and it is frequently said that their resignations are in accordance with the principles of ministerial responsibility, their resignations are normally related more to their relationship with their party and their Prime Minister, the sort of relationship which is concerned about their party's political fortunes. The resignations frequently have little or nothing to do with the Minister's responsibilities to the Parliament.

Another series of distortions of the ministerial responsibility system concern the relationship between Ministers and public servants. Australian Governments (federal and State) developed a method of drawing a line between a Minister's responsibility and the conduct of government administration by creating statutory authorities—government activities which were carried on under legislative authority which pushed them a step away from direct ministerial control, and more importantly made the Minister less responsible for their activities. Ministers were generally given power to direct various statutory authorities as to the policies they should adopt, but Ministers were not required to answer to Parliament for their administration.

But even ordinary Public Service departments have taken on

roles which suggest they have at times some independent authority. In the past decade or two, many heads of Public Service departments have become public figures, and their views have become well known, particularly when they are different from those of the Government which directs their work. Departments have in some cases leaked material to the media about differences over policy issues with Ministers, and Ministers have responded in similar ways. The result is that while Public Service departments are not meant to be independent at all, many of them have developed some autonomy and corporate character which Ministers may not always be able to control.

Ministerial responsibility has a different character in Australia from its theoretical model, but it does remain an important concept whose name is often summoned in political debate as though it was some inviolable principle at the heart of Government. The problem is that the Australian political system has not fully defined the place the concept really occupies in the Canberra system.

CHAPTER 19

Democracy in Action

Parliament, according to the textbook writers, has a formidable array of responsibilities. First, it determines which political party or group of parties will form the Government. These days it does this in a 'hands off' way—it is now automatic that the party or coalition of parties which win a majority of seats in the House of Representatives will form the Government without the need even for the Parliament to meet or, when it does meet, to vote its approval of the new Government. But the responsibility for deciding whether a Government remains in power stays with the Parliament throughout its life. A party or coalition split would see the fate of the Government being determined by the number of votes the various sides could muster in the House of Representatives.

A second function of the Parliament is to help determine party leadership. Ministers and shadow Ministers have to be Members of the Parliament. Performance on the floor of Parliament influences the way members of the various parliamentary parties vote in determining their leaders.

A third responsibility is to control government administration. By means of questions, debates and committee inquiries, the members of the Parliament try to keep a close eye on the activities of the Government and the Public Service.

A fourth responsibility is to supervise the government's financial administration, ensuring as far as possible that public money is not wasted, and that the Government's financial planning and administration are efficient. Again the Parliament has to rely on methods such as questions, debates and committee work to carry out its functions, but it is assisted by an independent Auditor-General and his staff.

The Parliament's major public role is to legislate—to pass the laws which implement the policies of the Government. Parliamentary members have largely surrendered the initiative in proposing laws to the Government. It is not unusual to hear the Parliament being accused of being a mere rubber stamp in the law making process.

Finally, the Parliament provides an important means by which political parties publicise political issues. It provides an institutional forum where Government and Opposition can challenge one another on day-to-day issues, and on their respective views of the national interest. But it depends on the media to perform this function effectively, and the media prefers to stage their own versions of the political battle.

An assessment of how the Commonwealth Parliament meets these theoretical objectives would depend on just when it was being measured. In the first ten years after the creation of the Commonwealth of Australia, the Parliament and its Members were extraordinarily active in passing laws to establish the institutions of the new nation, and in determining policy. Control of the Parliament was divided among three parties, with none of them able to obtain a majority at the elections in 1901, 1903 or 1906. Shifting allegiances and party deals within the House of Representatives determined which party would govern. But being in a minority position, no Government could be sure just which pieces of its legislative program would be passed by the Parliament, or how much its proposals would be amended. In those days the Parliament really did determine who would govern the country and it was the Parliament which decided which legislation would pass and in what form.

But the parliamentary scene changed as the political battle became a contest between the Labor Party and the anti-Labor coalitions. Party discipline increased, leaving little room for any expression in the Parliament of individual legislative initiatives. Government was determined largely by the result of elections and not by wheeling and dealing in the Parliament, though the Labor Party twice lost power through party splits, and non-Labor lost power once when its independent supporters deserted it.

Party discipline focused power into the hands of party leaders, particularly in the non-Labor parties. Governments generally controlled both the Senate and the House of Representatives, reducing the opportunity for successful legislative initiatives originating outside government.

A significant change in political and parliamentary styles and performances did not occur until the late 1960s, after the departure of Sir Robert Menzies who had dominated the political scene for sixteen years. The Senate demonstrated its desire to be more independent of the Government, establishing a vast number of committees, and taking a critical look at some Government legislation. This change was encouraged by a change in the party constitution of the Senate—the Government was most often without a majority of its own and dependent on minor parties or independents to see its legislative program through. At the same time the political parties became less amenable to rule by their leaders. In the 1970s and the 1980s these developments have been consolidated with changes in the Electoral Act which make it virtually impossible for any Government to win control of the Senate, and the development of party committees to the stage where consultation among all parliamentary members of a political party is virtually guaranteed, at least in relation to legislation which is to be considered by the Parliament. In fact, these are but two of a series of developments which have had a practical impact on the way the Commonwealth Parliament fulfils its functions.

One of the most important developments has been the move by the executive Government (the Ministers) into the Parliament building. In a physical, geographical sense, the notion of the separation of the executive from the legislature has been completely abandoned. But this has not led to any increased dominance by the executive over the Parliament, a complaint commonly voiced about the situation in Britain and other parliamentary democracies. Indeed, the location of Ministers in the parliament building has made them more accessible to all backbenchers (and the media) and has allowed Oppositions to resist calls for changes in the way Parliament operates so as to free Ministers of the need for their continuous attendance in the Parliament when it is sitting.

A second feature of the Commonwealth scene is the comparative smallness of the ministry and the Parliament—compared, that is, with other countries (and not with the States). The Australian House of Representatives has about 22 Ministers in a House with a total membership of less than 150. The British House of Commons has a Ministry four or five times the size of the Australian, drawn from a House with more than 600 Members. In Australia, parliamentarians are expected to devote themselves full-time to their duties, and the Chambers of the Parliament are designed to fit them all in. The atmosphere in both Houses in the old parliament building is reasonably intimate.

A third matter concerns the development of the party system.

Discipline in all political parties has become an end in itself. Voting in the Parliament is strictly along partly lines and any deviation is seized on by the media as a 'split' or a 'revolt'. The media's attitude has reinforced the pressures on MPs and Senators to follow their party's line. This pressure has also helped the development of identifiable factions within parties (e.g., left, socialist left, centre left, right in the ALP, wets and dries, and conservatives in the Liberal Party); as it has become more difficult for party members to identify their differences with party policies by voting against the party, they have had to find ways of showing that such differences exist within the ranks of the party.

A fourth factor has been the development of Canberra as the national capital, and Parliament House as the national centre of Government and Parliament. Canberra is very distant from the main centres of population in Australia; it is still regarded as a small, artificial town (despite its 1/4 million population); and the politicians and their bureaucratic advisers who operate out of Canberra are regarded as working in an 'ivory tower' atmosphere, quite foreign to the 'real' Australia. These sentiments tend to be shared by the politicians who, because of the working hours which are imposed on them, hardly ever venture outside the Parliament building. Time and distance and space have appeared to isolate the parliamentarians from their communities, although in fact they probably move among their constituents far more often than do British or American politicians.

Style and substance

Critics of the parliamentary system complain that it no longer plays its proper role in the political processes of the nation: it rubber stamps the legislation which is proposed by the Government and the Public Service; it discourages private Members from introducing legislation and rarely approves such Bills; it is dominated by the political leaders who also dominate the elections; it is overwhelmed by considerations of party, and individual MPs are no longer listened to and can make no impact on the party-determined outcome of everything that occurs in the Parliament; pressures of work and time mean that legislation is not properly debated or analysed; much law making has been delegated to the executive which through the making of regulations is able largely to by-pass parliamentary scrutiny; increased secrecy results in less information being made available on key issues of foreign policy and defence; the majority party appoints its members as chairmen of all committees thus reducing the likelihood of their work being truly independent of the Government; and the Parliament does not sit for long enough in each year.

Developments in the past decade or so have met many of these criticisms.

The committee system

The Senate has led the Parliament into developing a committee system which has the power both to investigate a vast area of government administration, and to influence beneficially the shape of legislation presented to the Parliament and regulations made by the executive. The committees mostly operate in a non-partisan way. They examine problems which otherwise might not be investigated by government agencies, and they probe policy making, expenditure and budgetary processes in a way which the Parliament as a whole is unable to do. Senate committees have established procedures to ensure that attention is drawn to legislation which might affect civil rights and the powers of government officials and Ministers.

Party committees

The parties represented in the Parliament have developed committee systems of their own, designed to ensure that party leaders, executives and Cabinets do not ignore the backbenchers who vote the party line in the Parliament. Policy making and the shaping of legislation has been democratised within each of the political parties in the Parliament. Backbenchers have more say in their party committees than they have ever had in the Parliament itself. And the party committees have shown a desire to bring outside advice to bear in their work, utilising the public service and non-governmental experts and interest groups. The development of party committees has its problems: they meet in private rather than in public and what they do tends to derogate from the role of the Parliament itself. But they give more power and influence to the vast mass of backbenchers who are elected to the Parliament and who previously were unable to influence either the laws they were expected to pass, or the policies of the Government they were there to support.

Information and expertise

Committee work has allowed MPs and Senators to specialise in areas of government of their own choosing. The facilities recently provided to them through the Parliamentary Library in particular have enabled them to develop some expertise within their specialties. Information is more available and more obtainable, even if government is becoming more complex. And parliamentarians have been provided with more staff to help them digest the material which is regularly provided to them by the Parliament, and which they seek out for themselves.

Slum clearance

The decision to construct a new Parliament building as part of the bicentenary celebrations has meant that the average MP or Senator is to cease to be housed in a way which has made it appear that he or she is a person of absolutely no consequence. The cramped offices in most of the old parliament building made the working lives of conscientious legislators extremely difficult, and would not have convinced any visitors that the parliamentarian played any significant role in the political life of the nation.

Reform

There are some problems for the Parliament which cannot be cured by the construction of a new building or the creation of new institutions such as committees. The federal nature of the Australian Commonwealth and the Constitution limits its powers and the way its conducts its business. There are some solutions to political problems which are beyond its legal reach. Such limitations as the Constitution imposes were a pre-condition to the very formation of the Australian nation, and the Australian people have shown a very great reluctance to agree in referendums to any significant changes in the system which was adopted in 1900. It could only be through a constitutional change that the Parliament could have fixed terms for the House of Representatives (a move which arguably would reduce the power of Prime Ministers). Only a constitutional change could reduce the power of the Senate. But other changes in the system are possible through legislative means (as the changes to the electoral system have demonstrated). And still others could be achieved by resolutions passed by the two Houses. Already the Parliament is considering changes to the laws which limit the broadcasting of proceedings, so as to encourage a greater appreciation of what the Parliament does. And the House of Representatives is considering changes in its procedure which would make what it does more easily understood. Such changes could also result in more time being made available to the Opposition and backbenchers to air their views and grievances, and help reduce the disruptions that occur through frustration.

Parliament's reputation suffers in part because of sheer ignorance about what it does and how it functions. Most school systems within Australia provide no courses which teach students about the nature of their governmental and parliamentary system. In 1985 the Electoral Office had a poll conducted to try to help it find an explanation for a substantial increase in informal voting in the 1984 House of Representatives election. It found that fewer than two-thirds of those sampled knew the names of the two Houses of the Federal Parliament, and only 60 per cent knew that the Prime Minister and the Leader of the Opposition were both Members of the House of Representatives and not the Senate. The media do not help to provide an understanding of even these most basic facts about the system. Frequently the shorthand 'Parliament' is used to refer to events which occurred in either the House of Representatives or the Senate. Media reports tend to concentrate on the more sensational aspects of what happens. And sensations are more concerned with the destructive aspects of parliamentary activity, and not with the constructive areas. The media see only the clashes which occur at the front of the parliamentary stage, and rarely focus on the activity of the mass of players who are performing their unspectacular but essential duties.

What is lost sight of is the pivotal importance of the Commonwealth Parliament in the national political system. Parliament alone provides the democratic link in the system. It belongs to the people, not to the Government, not to the state. In Britain the Parliament in the Palace of Westminster won its powers from the king slowly over the centuries. In Australia the parliamentary palace was built by the people. The Constitution of the Commonwealth begins by declaring that the people of the various colonies had agreed to unite in one indissoluble federal Commonwealth. This was not mere rhetoric; the proposals were approved in referendums of the people.

In the eighty-five years since the creation of the Commonwealth, the people's representatives have not always insisted that the Parliament should play its proper role in the political system. But the structure which they have created allows the Australian people to determine just how important their Parliament should be.

Index